John Miller

CONTACT
U.S.A.

Paul Abraham———————————————

Daphne Mackey———————————————

Boston University

CONTACT
U.S.A.

An ESL Reading and Vocabulary Textbook

Illustrated by Marci Davis

Prentice-Hall Inc., Englewood Cliffs, New Jersey 07632

Library of Congress Cataloging in Publication Data

ABRAHAM, PAUL,
  Contact U.S.A.

  1. English language—Text-books for
foreigners. I. Mackey, Daphne. II. Title.
PE1128.A27 1981   428.2′4   81-11898
ISBN 0-13-169599-1   AACR2

Interior design and editorial/
  production supervision by Chrys Chrzanowski
Cover design by Tony Ferrara Studio
Cover drawings by Marci Davis
Manufacturing buyer: Harry P. Baisley

Printed in the United States of America
10 9 8 7 6

ISBN 0-13-169599-1

PRENTICE-HALL INTERNATIONAL, INC., *London*
PRENTICE-HALL OF AUSTRALIA PTY. LIMITED, *Sydney*
PRENTICE-HALL OF CANADA, LTD., *Toronto*
PRENTICE-HALL OF INDIA PRIVATE LIMITED, *New Delhi*
PRENTICE-HALL OF JAPAN, INC., *Tokyo*
PRENTICE-HALL OF SOUTHEAST ASIA PTE. LTD., *Singapore*
WHITEHALL BOOKS LIMITED, WELLINGTON, *New Zealand*

To the Unsung Professionals of ESL

Contents

Introduction to the Teacher

Contact U.S.A. is a reading and vocabulary text for high-beginning and low-intermediate ESL students. Although its structure and exercises are aimed primarily at developing academic reading skills and vocabulary, its content (a look at changes in values and lifestyles in the United States) is highly appropriate for all non-native English speakers, including immigrants, students in higher educational institutions, and students of English in foreign countries.

READING

Reading for high-beginning and low-intermediate students is sometimes a frustrating experience. Books that are appropriate in terms of the students' active English proficiency are often not challenging for adult readers, either in structure or content. Readings that match the student's intellectual or conceptual interest level usually have exercises requiring a more advanced active English proficiency. We have written this book on the premise that adult students at this level of English proficiency are able to read and understand more in English than they are able to actively produce. Therefore, although the readings may appear to be difficult for students at this level at first glance, the first analytical exercises are relatively simple, requiring only passive reading and vocabulary skills. We feel that these types of reading and vocabulary skills are important for students to develop, particularly because the analysis of a reading beyond their proficiency level is a process that students confront in standardized tests in English. The reading exercises in this book progress from main idea to inference. The following is a general outline of each chapter.

CHAPTER OUTLINE

Section 1: A First Look
  A. Main Idea
  B. Reading
  C. Scanning
  D. Vocabulary (similar-different analysis of vocabulary in the context of the reading)
  E. Reading Comprehension (multiple choice)

Section 2: Look Again
- A. Vocabulary (multiple choice)
- B. Reading Comprehension (multiple choice)
- C. Questions (active comprehension analysis of reading)

Section 3: Contact a Point of View
- A. Timed Reading (a personal observation followed by True, False, or Impossible to Know statements)
- B. Vocabulary
- C. Word Forms (progressing through the book from recognition of function and form to production of appropriate forms)
- D. Speaking (semi-controlled discussion activities)
- E. Writing (controlled and free composition)

Section 4: Look Back
- A. Vocabulary (additional multiple choice)
- B. Matching (synonyms)

In addition, the book contains Reading Clues (questions in each chapter with answers and examples in the Appendix), Vocabulary Review Tests, and Answer Keys (both for chapter exercises and the review tests). There is also a Score Grid on which students may record their results for each section of each chapter.

VOCABULARY

This book was written with the firm belief that dictionaries are generally a reading inhibitor rather than a reading enhancer. With this in mind, the cardinal rule of the book is NO DICTIONARIES ALLOWED. The meaning of much of the vocabulary is implied within the reading passage, as the students discover when they complete the first vocabulary exercise, which requires them to analyze words within the context of the reading and compare them to other words that they already know. The vocabulary exercises and the inaccessibility of a dictionary force the students to look for meaning within the context, an essential reading skill. This book serves as a vocabulary builder because we reuse the vocabulary throughout the book so that students are forced to recall vocabulary from previous chapters, where it is used in different contexts. This leads to actual acquisition of the words in the text.

CONTENT

From our experience as teachers, we feel that adult language learners need stimulating reading materials that (1) provide them with background information about

American culture, (2) encourage their awareness of their environment, (3) prepare them to deal with the environment of the United States and, (4) let them draw their own conclusions about the United States. The presentation of information about the life and values in the United States is a very touchy subject; students are sensitive to "pro-America" rhetoric. In spite of this wariness, however, students want to understand some of the basic values and issues in the United States. We have chosen themes that have always generated a lot of discussion in class and about which students have strong opinions. The focus of these readings is primarily cross-cultural. The readings enable students and the teacher to examine American culture, to evaluate their feelings, and to redefine their positions in this culture or in their own cultures. We have tried to present, as far as possible, an apolitical portrayal of the United States. The first reading in every chapter is general, giving the overall idea and the key vocabulary items connected to the subject. The second reading (the timed reading) is a personal point of view about some aspect of the subject. For example, the second timed reading in the chapter on immigration is from the point of view of a native American. The chapter on race issues has a second reading about reverse discrimination. These points of view are closely tied in with the speaking activities in each chapter, encouraging students to express their ideas about the subject. Since these readings are our personal impressions, and are, as such, debatable, we encourage teachers to feel free to contribute their own personal points of view and to express their cultural perspectives.

SUGGESTIONS FOR USING CONTACT U.S.A.

Chapter 1 is written as an introduction to the students. We suggest that teachers use it to orient the students to the book. In-class use will assure that all students understand the procedures and directions for the exercises.

Answer keys are included at the ends of the chapters and Review Tests.

Individualization is possible since the students can use the answer keys to correct their own exercises. The only exercises that the students must do together are the speaking activities and the timed readings (unless provisions can be made to have students do the timed readings individually).

Review tests are included in order to test vocabulary acquisition. They cover three chapters each (except for the final test) and test the words in different contexts than those in which the words appear in the readings. The sentences are similar to the test items in standardized tests.

Once again, teachers should emphasize the fact that *no dictionaries* are to be used. This book has been written with the intention of teaching vocabulary: The exercises in each chapter are designed as learning tools for the students; the review tests are designed to test vocabulary acquisition. Therefore, teachers should expect the students to make few mistakes. Teachers can monitor students' progress by checking the score grids at the end of the book. On these grids, students will record the number of mistakes that they make in each section of the chapter. The teachers should look for sections that individual students have difficulties with and suggest ways for them to improve their work in these sections. Students will also record the total number of mistakes for each chapter. These scores can be interpreted as follows:

0–5 mistakes: Excellent
6–10 mistakes: Good
11–14 mistakes: Student needs to review the sections that presented difficulties.
Over 15 mistakes: Student needs to do chapter again.
Some students may find the first few chapters easy. Teachers should use their own discretion in assessing the needs of the students.

EACH CHAPTER

Section 1: It is a good idea to do Section One during class time, at least at the beginning, so that you can check that students do not use the dictionary and that they work at a reasonable pace.

A. Main Idea: Give the students about one and a half to two minutes to find the main idea of the reading. Correct this exercise before students go on to Exercise B.

B. Reading: This is a general reading that gives background information and vocabulary. We suggest that the students work at their own paces in this section. Encourage students not to follow the text with their pencils, mouth the words as they read, or fixate on unknown vocabulary items.

C. Scanning: In order to emphasize reading skills, this exercise may be done before Exercise B and be timed. This exercise is used to give students practice in finding specific information quickly.

D. Vocabulary: This exercise is used to help students determine the meaning of unfamiliar words by examining them in context. Encourage the students to find the words in the reading (the line numbers are given after the words in the exercise). Also emphasize the fact that the term *similar* is not exact—it refers to general similarity.

E. Reading Comprehension: It is not necessary to go over the answers to the multiple choice exercises unless the students have specific questions. They should be able to find the correct answers. In addition, they have a further look at the reading comprehension exercise in Section 2.

CORRECT THE ANSWERS FOR SECTION 1 BEFORE GOING ON TO SECTION 2.

Section 2: After the students have graded their answers to Section 1, they can go on to this more detailed look at the reading.

A. Vocabulary: The students may find it helpful to look back at the reading or at the vocabulary exercise in Section 1 in order to complete this vocabulary exercise. Again, no dictionaries may be used.

B. Reading Comprehension: In this last multiple choice reading comprehension check, students should get 90% of the questions correct.

C. Questions: These questions may be written or done orally. They serve as a comprehension check, to make sure that the students understand the general meaning of the reading. Students often give too much information when they do this exercise because they lift exact sentences from the reading instead of the specific and limited information required by the question. Therefore, it is helpful to ask the students to do the exercise with their books open, but then ask them to give the answers in class with their books closed. When they try to answer from memory, they are more likely to give only the essential information.

Section 3: This section presents a point of view connected to the subject of the chapter. This point of view is used first as a timed reading, but teachers are encouraged to use it for discussion.

A. Timed Reading: The four-minute time limit is a general guideline. Teachers should feel free to vary it according to the reading abilities of their students. The questions following the timed reading are to be done in the four-minute limit also. The students may want to read the questions first and then scan the reading quickly to find the answers. They are asked to decide if the statements are true, false, or impossible to know from the information and implications given in the reading.

B. Vocabulary: This vocabulary exercise varies from chapter to chapter in form, but tests the vocabulary given in the timed reading.

C. Word Forms: These word form exercises follow a progression from recognition of differences in the function and form of words in sentences to production of the proper forms. Following is an outline of this section through the book:

> Chapters 1, 2 and 3: Recognition of the function of adjectives, nouns, and verbs
> Chapters 4, 5, and 6: Suffixes for adjectives; recognition of adjectives, verbs, and nouns
> Chapter 7: Production of the appropriate forms of adjectives or nouns
> Chapter 8: Suffixes for nouns
> Chapter 9: Production of nouns and adjectives
> Chapter 10: Production and discrimination of nouns, adjectives, and verbs
> Chapters 11 and 12: Function and recognition of adverbs and adjectives
> Chapters 12 and 14: Review of all forms requiring production

D. Speaking: The speaking activities in the book vary in each chapter. They may be general discussion questions, role plays, or problem-solving exercises. All of them serve to initiate discussion and to provide the students with the necessary vocabulary or forms essential for the discussion. While doing these activities, the students will require the vocabulary introduced in the chapters.

E. Writing: The writing activities are connected either to the speaking exercises or to the reading clues. They include both controlled and free composition as well as sentence combining and sentence completion exercises. Some of the writing exercises require additional grammatical explanations by the teacher; for example, in Chapter 10, an understanding of the modal auxiliaries is necessary for completion of this exercise.

Section 4: Section four is a review of the vocabulary in the chapter. If students do poorly on the exercises in this section, they should go back and study the vocabulary again.

 A. Vocabulary: Multiple choice questions test knowledge of the vocabulary in the chapter.

 B. Matching: The matching exercise tests vocabulary by asking the students to find synonyms for words.

Introduction to the Student

Contact U.S.A. has two purposes:

1. to improve your READING ability, and
2. to improve your VOCABULARY.

Each chapter in the book has:

A First Look: exercises to determine general meaning of reading and vocabulary items.
      A. Main Idea
      B. Reading
      C. Scanning
      D. Vocabulary (similar/different)
      E. Reading Comprehension

Look Again: more detailed exercises in reading comprehension and vocabulary
      A. Vocabulary
      B. Reading Comprehension
      C. Questions

Contact a Point of View: a second reading:
      A. Timed Reading Exercise
      B. Vocabulary
      C. Word Forms
      D. Speaking
      E. Writing

Look Back: review of the vocabulary from the chapter:
      A. Vocabulary
      B. Matching

The first chapter, "Impressions of the United States," has special instructions for each exercise. These instructions will teach you how to use the book effectively.

chapter 1

Impressions
of the United States

A First Look

Before you begin to read, it is important to have a general idea about the subject of the reading. One way to get this overview is to understand the title of the reading, for example, "Impressions of the United States." Another way is to look at the pictures or illustrations in the chapter.

After you have a general idea (from the title and the illustrations), you need to look at the reading itself. In English, written work is divided into paragraphs. A *paragraph* is a group of sentences with one general meaning. There are five paragraphs in the reading, "Impressions of the United States," which follows. Can you find them?

1. What is the first word in the third paragraph?
2. What is the last word in the fourth paragraph?

The answer to question 1 is *these*. The answer to question 2 is *friendships*. The paragraphs in this book have numbers on the left. Remember that when you use numbers before a noun, as in 1 paragraph, you use the words (1) first, (2) second, (3) third, (4) fourth, (5) fifth, (6) sixth, (7) seventh, (8) eighth, (9) ninth, and (10) tenth. So, you say *first paragraph*. Now, find the main idea of each paragraph in the reading. Do exercise A.

A. Main Idea

DIRECTIONS: *Before you begin to read, look at these main ideas. There is one main idea for each paragraph. Write the number of the paragraph next to the main idea of that paragraph. Work very quickly. Do not read every word at this point.*

1. __2__ positive and negative ideas about the United States

2. __4__ knowledge of a country

3. __5__ this book about the United States

4. __1__ first thoughts about the United States

5. __3__ how people form impressions

B. Reading

DIRECTIONS: Now read carefully, but try to think about groups of words, not individual words. Do not stop if you do not know the meaning of a word.

1	The United States. What is your first thought when you hear these words? Is it an image of something typically American?* Perhaps you think of hamburgers and fast-food restaurants. Or perhaps you have an image of a product, such as an American car. Some people immediately think of American universities. Others think of American companies. Many Americans think of the red, white, and blue flag when they think of the United States. There are many images associated with the name of a country.	1 2 3 4 5 6 7 8

There are also many ideas or concepts associated with the words *United States*. Some people think of a positive concept, such as freedom, when they think of the United States. Other people think of a negative concept, such as imperialism, the political and economic control of another country by a government. Many Americans have both positive and negative ideas about their country. When they think of the lifestyle or the scenery (landscapes such as mountains or beaches at the ocean), they feel very positive and proud of their country. But sometimes, when they think about the government, they think about taxes and inflation. Then they have negative feelings about the country. — 9–19

These images and ideas are all impressions of a country, the United States. People form these impressions in many different ways. They see American products and advertisements. They read newspapers and hear people talk about the United States. They probably see American movies and television shows. These impressions are always changing. As people receive more information, they alter their images and concepts of a country. — 20–26

Knowledge of a country includes many things. Typical products and actions by governments are part of this knowledge. But the most important thing in learning about a country is knowledge of the people of that country. What are their customs and lifestyles? How do they raise their children? What are their values and beliefs? How do they feel about work and entertainment, about time, about friendships? — 27–33

In this book you will read about many aspects of the United States. You will read about lifestyles, institutions, values, and issues — 34–35

---

* Although technically more accurate, the term *North American* is not used by the people in the United States to describe themselves. Therefore, the term *American* is used throughout this book to describe things in the United States.

5   which are all part of American life and culture. Before you begin   *36*
           each chapter, think of your own impressions of the subject, American   *37*
           women, American cities, American families. Use your own impres-   *38*
           sions to compare with and question the impressions of the authors.   *39*
           Contact the U.S.A.   *40*

Reading Clue

1.1   What does "such as" in lines 10 and 11 introduce?
       (a) a definition
       (b) an example
       (c) a reason
Look at page 223 for the answer.

It is important to be able to find information quickly. This is <u>scanning</u>. Do the next exercise as quickly as possible.

C. Scanning

DIRECTIONS: *Write the number of the paragraph where you find the following information.*

a. _____1_____ red, white, and blue

b. _____3_____ American movies and television shows

c. _____1_____ fast-food restaurants

d. _____5_____ contact the U.S.A.

e. _____3_____ see American products and advertisements

f. _____4_____ values and beliefs

g. _____2_____ scenery and landscapes

h. _____5_____ before you begin each chapter

i. _____2_____ taxes and inflation

j. _____3_____ read the newspaper

The following vocabulary exercise will help you understand the meaning of new words in the reading without a dictionary.

Example: car (4)   **automobile**   _similar_

Find "car" in line 4 of the reading. Look at the words and sentences around it. Is the meaning of *car* similar to or different from the meaning of *automobile*? The meanings of *car* and *automobile* are similar. So, you write *similar* on the line. Remember that the word *similar* does not mean exactly the same; it means that two things are close in meaning.

Now try another example: first (1)   **last**   _different_

Are the words similar or different? The meanings are different, so you write *different* on the line. Now go on to exercise D.

D. Vocabulary

DIRECTIONS: *Look at the following pairs of words. Find the word on the left in the reading. Compare its meaning to the word(s) on the right. Are the words similar or different? Write similar or different on the line.*

thought (1)	idea	1. _S_
image (2)	picture	2. _S_
perhaps (2-3)	maybe	3. _S_
ideas (9)	concepts	4. _S_
positive (10, 14)	negative (12, 14)	5. _D_
scenery (15)	landscapes (15)	6. _S_
impressions (20)	first ideas	7. _S_
form (21)	make	8. _S_
include (27)	have inside	9. _S_
typical (27)	usual	10. _S_
products (22-27)	customs	11. _D_
aspects (34)	sides	12. _S_
lifestyle (15-35)	institutions (35)	13. _D_
compare with (39)	look at side by side	14. _S_
question (39)	answer	15. _D_

How much of the reading did you understand without using a dictionary? Do the next exercise to find out.

E. Reading Comprehension

DIRECTIONS: Circle the letter of the choice that best completes each sentence.

1. There are ____ examples given of images associated with the name *United States*.

   a. five   b. six   c. seven

2. The ____ is red, white, and blue.

   a. colored TV   b. landscape   c. flag

3. Knowledge of a country includes knowledge of typical products, governmental action, and ____.

   a. the people   b. information   c. children

4. Americans feel ____ when they think of the American government, taxes, and inflation.

   a. proud   b. negative   c. positive

5. An example of a negative concept is ____.

   a. social work   b. imperialism   c. the American flag

6. According to the author, imperialism is ____ control.

   a. social   b. racial   c. political and economic

7. An example of a positive concept is ____.

   a. inflation   b. freedom   c. automobiles

8. According to the author, people's ideas about a country ____.

   a. change often   b. are always the same   c. are always derived from TV and movies

9. The term *American* is used because ____.

   a. North American is too long   b. people in the United States use it   c. the book is about Canada

10. According to the author, Americans ____ think bad things about their country.

   a. always   b. never   c. sometimes

Look Again

Look at the corrected answers for the vocabulary exercise (exercise D) in section 1. Use the <u>similar</u> words to understand the meanings and to answer this vocabulary exercise. If the words in the following exercise are not in exercise D, look for them in the reading in order to understand their meanings. Do not use a dictionary.

A. Vocabulary

DIRECTIONS: Circle the letter of the choice that bests completes each sentence.

1. I want to know more about the ____ of the people: what they do every day and how they spend their free time.

   a. work   b. lifestyle   c. products

2. My mother and my father work; ____ of my parents work.

   a. friendships   b. some   c. both

3. After work, I like to go out for some ____.

   a. entertainment   b. impressions   c. customs

4. Some people are happy about the changes, but ____ are unhappy.

   a. institutions   b. personals   c. others

5. On the train I looked out the window at the ____.

   a. scenery   b. products   c. customs

6. There are many different ____ to the problem. It is not easy to understand.

   a. images   b. aspects   c. people

7. Schools and churches are ____.

   a. lifestyles   b. institutions   c. landscapes

8. The color ____ on this TV is not very good.

   a. impression   b. concept   c. image

9. Problems with the government are ____ problems.

a. positive   b. political   c. associated with

10. The two men work in different fields of study. They are not ____ each other.

a. associated with   b. customs   c. political

B. Reading Comprehension

DIRECTIONS: Circle the letter of the choice that best completes each sentence.

1. In paragraph 5, the author gives the idea that your ideas will ____.   *"...to compare with and question..."*

a. always be the same
   as the author's ideas
     b. sometimes be different
   from the author's ideas
     c. be wrong

2. ____ is an example of a positive concept.

a. Inflation   b. Freedom   c. Politics

3. Lifestyles, institutions, values, and beliefs are all ____ American culture.

a. life in   b. impressions of   c. aspects of

4. Foreign business people probably think of an American ____ when they hear the words *United States*.

a. product   b. advertisement   c. university

5. The author thinks that you, the reader, have ____ the United States already.

a. no knowledge of   b. many impressions of   c. negative ideas about

6. According to the author, imperialism is ____.

a. political control in
   the United States
     b. no longer happening   c. a negative concept

7. According to the article, Americans are ____ about their lifestyle.

a. happy   b. unhappy   c. negative

8. Inflation is a(n) ____.

a. impression   b. economic problem   c. positive idea

9. ____ are typically American.

a. Cars   b. Hamburgers   c. Universities

10. According to the author, Americans are proud of ____ in their country.

a. taxes   b. the scenery   c. freedom

C. Questions

DIRECTIONS: Answer the following questions.

1. Give two examples of fast-food restaurants.

2. What is imperialism?

3. What does the author think is most important to learn about a country?

4. What are some of the subjects in this book?

5. Why does the author use the term *American* instead of *North American*?

Contact a Point of View

Reading quickly is a very important skill. Remember to read groups of words—do not stop on individual words. You must read <u>and</u> complete the first exercise in four minutes, so you need to read <u>very</u> quickly. The statements in the exercise contain information connected to the reading. This information is either *true* or *false* or it is *impossible to know* (because the reading does not give that information).

A. Timed Reading

> DIRECTIONS: Read the following point of view and answer the questions in four minutes.

(handwritten margin notes: informality, jogger, profession, respect)

I am from Thailand. I am a student in an American university. This is my third year in the United States. After three years, it is difficult to remember my first impressions of the United States. But I noticed then and still notice now how much more informality there is in the United States than there is in Thailand.

Take, for example, clothes. I expected to see blue jeans because this is where they started, isn't it? But I didn't expect to see so many old blue jeans. I also didn't expect to see running shoes worn in classes, downtown, and even in expensive restaurants! I also couldn't believe the runners, joggers they call them, all over the place, but that gets into how Americans feel about health, which is another interesting concept.

If you think about the English language, you know that it is not a formal language. There is only one *you* and not a formal *you* for older people and an informal *you* for friends and children. I remember another thing that surprised me. My first English teacher in the United States was about fifty years old, but we called him *Al*, his first name. I wanted to call him Mr. Al, but he didn't like that. But not all situations are informal like this; in business and in certain professions like medicine things are more formal.

As a young person, I like the American idea of informality, but I think it will be better to be old in Thailand where people respect old people and have more formal relationships.

DIRECTIONS: *Read each of the following statements carefully to determine whether each is true, false, or impossible to know. Check the appropriate blank.*

	TRUE	FALSE	IMPOSSIBLE TO KNOW
1. The writer is a woman.			✓
2. The writer is a university student.	✓		
3. Al was the teacher's last name.		✓	
4. The writer is young.	✓		
5. The writer is married.			✓
6. The writer never saw running shoes downtown.		✓	
7. The writer lived in the city of San Francisco.			✓
8. Americans call doctors by their first names.		✓	

	TRUE	FALSE	IMPOSSIBLE TO KNOW
9. The writer has more ideas about Americans and health.	✓		
10. The writer thinks formality is better for old people.	✓		

B. Vocabulary

DIRECTIONS: Circle the letter of the word(s) with the same meaning as the italicized word.

1. The way Americans feel about informality is an interesting *concept*.

   a. information (b.) idea c. aspect

2. I *noticed* a person sitting alone in the restaurant.

   (a.) saw b. talked to c. called

3. I know a lot of *runners*.

   a. bicycles b. office people (c.) joggers

4. They had a very old *friendship*.

   (a.) kind of relationship b. understanding c. belief

5. I have a good *impression* of her.

   (a.) general idea b. custom c. friendship

6. I never *start* my homework until 10:00 P.M.

   a. end (b.) begin c. try

7. Please give me *more* information.

   (a.) additional b. good c. better

8. I never *question* my father's ideas.

   a. answer b. understand (c.) ask about with doubt

9. This is an interesting *thought*.

   a. issue (b.) quick idea c. feeling

10. When my mother telephoned, I *immediately* told her the news.

    (a.) at the first moment b. generally c. slowly

C. Word Forms

DIRECTIONS: Read the following information about nouns and adjectives and then complete the exercise. Decide whether the italicized words are nouns or adjectives.

A *noun* is a word used to name something. For example, *girl, box, idea,* and *restaurant* are all nouns.

An *adjective* gives some information about a noun. For example, *good, interesting,* and *green* are all adjectives when they describe a noun.

	NOUN	ADJECTIVE
1. I live in a *small* apartment.	____	✔
2. *English* is difficult.	✓	____
3. I am studying *English* history.	✓	⬯
4. That is a *great* idea!	____	✓
5. Many good things in life are *free*.	____	✓
6. I have a *negative* feeling about politics.	____	✓
7. *Good* friends are life's greatest pleasure.	____	✓
8. I never read the *newspaper* here.	✓	____
9. Is that a typical *product* of your country?	✓	____
10. My aunt is one of the *friendliest* people I know.	____	✓

D. Speaking

DIRECTIONS: Share your ideas with a classmate or with the class. Complete the following sentences.

1. I expect(ed) to see . . . in the United States.

2. My impressions of the country are . . .

3. The most surprising thing about the United States is . . .

4. The thing which is most different for me . . .

5. Some examples of informality are . . .

E. Writing

For example and *such as* both introduce examples. *Such as* is always within a sentence. *For example* can be used at the beginning of the sentence. The punctuation is different for the two because *for example* must be separated from the rest of the sentence.

Examples: It is difficult to learn American idioms such as *waste time* and *spend time.*

It is difficult to learn American idioms. For example, what is the difference between *waste time* and *spend time?*

DIRECTIONS: Fill in the blanks with <u>such as</u> or <u>for example</u>.

1. I think that television has some positive things _____ educational shows for children.

2. American TV has a lot of commercials. Last night, _____ , there were twelve commercials on in thirty minutes.

3. I like team sports _____ soccer, basketball, and baseball.

4. I read a lot of magazines: _____ , *Vogue, Harper's,* and *Time.*

5. An international airport _____ LaGuardia in New York has thousands of people passing through it each day.

6. The word *American* has different meanings in different places; _____ _____ , in South America it means South Americans, but in North America it means North Americans.

7. If you have trouble sleeping at night, maybe you should watch what you eat. _____ , you shouldn't drink coffee, tea, or soda before you go to bed at night.

8. Drinks _____ hot milk or wine make you sleepy.

9. There are a lot of things we can do tonight. _____ , we can go to the movies or to the disco. What do you want to do?

10. Some things, _____ , freedom and health, are things you never think about until you do not have them anymore.

Look Back

A. Vocabulary

DIRECTIONS: Circle the letter of the choice that best completes each sentence.

1. I think that business is the best ____ to get into.

   a. lifestyle   b. profession   c. thought

2. My friend works in the government because she enjoys ____ .

   a. politics   b. production   c. advertisement

3. I am interested in this car because I like the ____ .

   a. impression   b. advertisement   c. flag

4. Some political people have a lot of ____ . They are very strong.

   a. control   b. imperialism   c. issues

5. I like the ____ in the mountains better than at the ocean.

   a. scenery   b. comparison   c. positive

6. What do you do for ____ ? Do you go to movies or stay at home?

   a. work   b. entertainment   c. association

7. I study at an English language ____ .

   a. situation   b. institute   c. profession

8. We pay ____ to the government.

   a. products   b. taxes   c. inflation

9. I don't have any ____ about the trip to New York.

   a. information   b. aspects   c. images

10. He did very strange things. His ____ frightened me.

    a. aspects   b. thoughts   c. actions

B. Matching

DIRECTIONS: *Find the word or phrase in column B that has a similar meaning to a word in column A. Write the letter of that word or phrase next to the word in column A.*

A

1. __*d*__ immediately
2. __*g*__ thought
3. _____ inflation
4. _____ alter
5. _____ jogger
6. _____ lifestyle
7. _____ positive
8. _____ landscape
9. _____ perhaps
10. _____ tax

B

a. economic problem
b. good
c. money paid to government
d. right away
e. scenery
f. change
g. idea
h. way of life
i. maybe
j. runner

chapter 2

A Country of Immigrants

A First Look

A. Main Idea

DIRECTIONS: Before you begin to read, look at these main ideas. There is one main idea for each paragraph. Write the number of the paragraph next to the main idea of that paragraph. Work very quickly. Do not read every word at this point.

1. _____3_____ examples of different types of neighborhoods

2. _____1_____ the different faces of immigrants in the United States

3. _____4_____ diversity in American society

4. _____2_____ history of immigration in the United States

B. Reading

DIRECTIONS: Now read carefully.

1   As you walk along the street in any American city, you see   1
many different faces. You see Oriental faces, black faces, and white   2
faces. These are the faces of the United States, a country of immi-   3
grants from all over the world. Immigrants are people who leave   4
one country to live permanently in another country.   5

2   The first immigrants came to North America in the 1600s from   6
northern European countries such as England and Holland. These   7
people generally had light skin and light hair. They came to live in   8
North America because they wanted religious freedom. In the 1700s   9
and early 1800s immigrants continued to move from Europe to the   10
United States. At this time there was one group of unwilling im-   11
migrants, black Africans. These people were tricked or forced to   12
come to the United States, where they worked on the large farms   13
in the south. The blacks had no freedom; they were slaves. In the   14
1800s many Chinese and Irish immigrants came to the United   15
States. They came because of economic or political problems in their   16

countries. The most recent immigrants to the United States, the   17
Cubans and Indochinese, also came because of economic or political   18
problems in their own countries. Except for the blacks, most of these   19
immigrants thought of the United States as a land of opportunity,   20
of a chance for freedom and new lives.   21

    In the United States, these immigrants looked for assistance   22
from other immigrants who shared the same background, language,   23
and religion. Therefore, there are neighborhoods in each U.S. city   24
made up almost entirely of one special group. There are all Italian,   25
all Puerto Rican, or all Irish neighborhoods in many East Coast   26
cities and all Mexican neighborhoods in the Southwest. There are   27
racial neighborhoods such as oriental Chinatown in San Francisco   28
and black Harlem in New York. There are also neighborhoods with   29
a strong religious feeling such as a Jewish part of Brooklyn in New   30
York. And, of course, there are economic neighborhood divisions; in   31
American cities very often poor people do not live in the same neigh-   32
borhoods as rich people.   33

    This diversity of neighborhoods in the cities is a reflection of   34
the different groups in American society. American society is a   35
mixture of various racial, language, cultural, religious, and eco-   36
nomic groups. People sometimes call America a *melting pot* and   37
compare its society to a soup with many different ingredients. The   38
ingredients (different races, cultures, religions, and economic groups)   39
are supposedly mixed together smoothly. But, in reality, there are   40
a few lumps left in the soup.   41

3

4

Reading Clues

2.1 What word in line 19 introduces one thing that is
different from other things? *Except for*
Look at page 223 for the answer.

2.2 What word in line 40 introduces a contrast, or a
different idea? *But*
Look at page 223 for the answer.

C. Scanning

*DIRECTIONS: Write the number of the paragraph (1-4) where you find the
following information.*

a. _____ light skin and light hair

b. _____ Mexican neighborhoods

c. _____ a country of immigrants

d. _____ most recent immigrants

e. _____ economic neighborhood divisions

f. _____ San Francisco

g. _____ live permanently in another country

h. _____ a *melting pot*

i. _____ white faces

j. _____ early 1800s

D. Vocabulary

DIRECTIONS: *Look at the following pairs of words. Find the word on the left in the reading. Compare its meaning to the word(s) on the right. Are the words similar or different? Write* similar *or* different *on the line.*

Example: black   **white**   *different*

           water   **H₂O**   *similar*

immigrants (4)	tourists	1. _____
such as (7)	for example	2. _____
generally (8)	usually	3. _____
unwilling (11)	willing	4. _____
slaves (14)	free people	5. _____
recent (17)	new	6. _____
except for (19)	but	7. _____
opportunity (20)	chance	8. _____
assistance (22)	help	9. _____
share (23)	have together	10. _____
neighborhoods (24)	cities	11. _____
entirely (25)	all	12. _____

poor (32)	rich (33)	13. _____
diversity (34)	variety	14. _____
supposedly (40)	in reality (40)	15. _____

E. Reading Comprehension

DIRECTIONS: Circle the letter of the choice that best completes each sentence.

1. Immigrants are ____ .

   a. countries b. neighborhoods c. people

2. The first immigrants in the United States were ____ .

   a. black b. religious people c. Indochinese

3. The black Africans in North America were ____ immigrants.

   a. happy b. unwilling c. recent

4. Many people came to the United States for ____ .

   a. freedom b. farms c. boats

5. Immigrants moved ____ other immigrants from their countries.

   a. close to b. far away from c. without

6. The most recent immigrants came because of ____ problems.

   a. racial b. religious c. political

7. In an American city there ____ .

   a. are many diverse neighborhoods b. is always a Mexican neighborhood c. are two neighborhoods

8. The main idea of the third paragraph is ____ .

   a. immigration b. American society c. neighborhoods in American cities

9. There are more ____ immigrants in the East.

   a. Irish b. Chinese c. Mexican

10. American society is ____ .

    a. mixed b. not completely mixed c. not mixed at all

Look Again

A. Vocabulary

DIRECTIONS: Circle the letter of the choice that best completes each sentence.

1. Assistance is ____ .

    a. religion   b. work   c. help

2. The East Coast and the Southwest are ____ of(in) the country.

    a. groups of people   b. parts   c. cities

3. An example of religion is ____ .

    a. Jewish   b. white   c. Italian

4. A neighborhood is ____ .

    a. an apartment building   b. a house   c. a city division

5. A society is ____ .

    a. a group of people   b. immigrants   c. all American

6. An example of race is ____ .

    a. Roman Catholic   b. white   c. Irish

7. A government problem is a ____ problem.

    a. political   b. street   c. forced

8. English is a ____ .

    a. language   b. religion   c. literature

9. A minute is a ____ of an hour.

    a. mixture   b. group   c. division

10. A person with a lot of money is ____ .

    a. economic   b. rich   c. poor

B. Reading Comprehension

DIRECTIONS: Circle the letter of the choice that best completes each sentence.

1. ____ immigrants came to the United States.

   a. Many   b. Few   c. Some

2. Two people of the same race share the same ____.

   a. language   b. religion   c. color

3. Irish and Mexican are ____.

   a. cities   b. nationalities   c. religions

4. Harlem is an example of a ____ neighborhood.

   a. religious   b. language   c. racial

5. American society is a mixture of different races, nationalities, religions, and ____.

   a. economic levels   b. countries   c. slaves

6. ____ immigrants came to the United States most recently.

   a. Northern European   b. Indochinese   c. Black

7. The Chinese and Irish immigrants came to the United States for ____.

   a. religious freedom   b. assistance   c. economic or political
                                                                 reasons

8. There are many Mexicans in ____.

   a. Boston   b. the Southwest   c. the North

9. There ____ rich and poor people in the same neighborhoods in the United States.

   a. are often   b. are not usually   c. are never

10. The main idea of the reading is ____.

    a. diversity in the   b. religious freedom   c. a country of opportunity
       United States

C. Questions

DIRECTIONS: Answer the following questions.

1. Who were the first immigrants to North America?

2. Who worked on large farms in the South?

3. Why did the Chinese and Irish immigrants come to the United States?

4. What is an example of a racial neighborhood?

5. Is the United States like a broth (a smooth soup) or like a vegetable soup?

Contact a Point of View

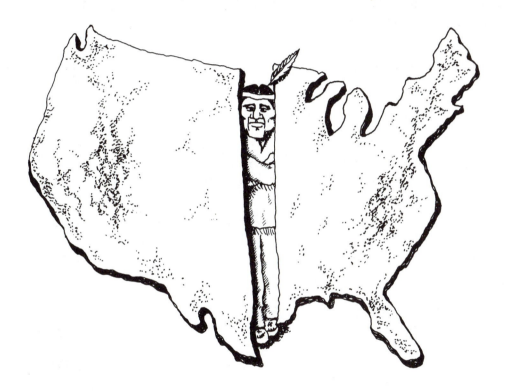

A. Timed Reading

DIRECTIONS: Read the following point of view and answer the questions in four minutes.

My name is Haske Noswood. I am a native American, a Navajo. You probably know native Americans as "Indians" and associate us with cowboys and western movies.

Most people forget that we were the first Americans, that we were here before any white men. Once, the Navajo and other native American groups lived well. Some of us hunted; some of us farmed. Most of us

downfall

moved from place to place according to the season. We did not believe in land ownership. This was our downfall. We believed that land belonged to all people.

The white people thought differently. They came to our lands and divided it up among themselves. They took our land. We did not understand until it was too late. They tricked us and forced us all onto these reservations. They "gave" us this reservation land. There is reservation land all over the country. There is the Hopi reservation in Arizona and the Cherokee reservation in Tennessee. But this reservation land is almost always the worst land. They put us on land that no one else wanted.

A lot of people have left the reservation to get good jobs or education. But I am staying on the reservation because my people have many problems now and I want to help them.

DIRECTIONS: Read each of the following statements carefully to determine whether each is true, false, or impossible to know. Check the appropriate blank.

	TRUE	FALSE	IMPOSSIBLE TO KNOW
1. A reservation is a city.		✓	
2. The Navajo reservation is in New Mexico.			✓
3. The Cherokee reservation is in Arizona.		✓	
4. High taxes are one of the problems on the reservation.			✓
5. The Navajo are rich.		✓	
6. Haske Noswood lives in New Mexico.			✓
7. All native Americans live in one area of the country.		✓	
8. The reservation land is bad land.	✓		
9. Each native American owned a piece of land.		✓	
10. Haske is a hunter.			✓

B. Vocabulary

DIRECTIONS: *Circle the letter of the word(s) with the same meaning as the italicized word(s).*

1. What is the *real* problem?

   a. true   b. bad   c. difficult

2. I was *once* a farmer.

   a. never   b. always   c. at one time

3. This is *the worst* weather! It is really cold.

   a. very bad   b. very difficult   c. amazing

4. Spending money was my *downfall*.

   a. happiness   b. opportunity   c. biggest problem

5. He did *poorly* on his test.

   a. badly   b. well   c. hard

6. We will *divide* the house into apartments.

   a. sell   b. cut up   c. live

7. The farming *season* in the north is very short.

   a. place   b. time of year   c. area

8. I will *call* the baby John.

   a. number   b. tell   c. name

9. I *force* myself to study.

   a. push   b. continue   c. walk

10. I live *well* but I have little money.

   a. in a good way   b. poorly   c. hard

C. Word Forms

DIRECTIONS: *Are the italicized words used as nouns or as adjectives?*

	NOUN	ADJECTIVE
1. Salt is an *ingredient* used in cooking.	_____	_____
2. That is quite a *wealthy* neighborhood.	_____	_____
3. What is your *problem*?	_____	_____

	NOUN	ADJECTIVE
4. He is a *native* of the United States.	_____	_____
5. My *native* language is English.	_____	_____
6. There is a large *group* of people outside.	_____	_____
7. What's the *difference*?	_____	_____
8. This is *your* book, isn't it?	_____	_____
9. What *color* is your hair?	_____	_____
10. My eyes are *brown*.	_____	_____

D. Speaking

DIRECTIONS: Share your ideas with a classmate or with the class. Answer the following questions.

1. Who were the first people in your country?

2. How many different groups of people are there in your country now?

3. What is(are) the language(s) in your country?

4. What is(are) the race(s) in your country?

5. What is(are) the religion(s) in your country?

E. Writing

The word *but* separates two different ideas. It is a conjunction; that is, it separates two groups of words which both contain a subject and a verb. For example,

water
vegetables
coffee
salt

Water, vegetables, and salt are ingredients in soup, *but* coffee is not.

Except for introduces one item or two that are different from the rest of a group.

All of these are ingredients in soup *except for* coffee.

*DIRECTIONS: For each of the following groups, complete two sentences.
Use <u>but</u> and <u>except for</u>.*

1. A   All of these are . . .

   t

   M   A, M, and Y are . . .

   Y

2. the Pacific   All of these are . . .

   the Amazon

   the Nile   The Ohio, the . . .

   the Ohio

3. a nickel   All of these are . . .

   a dime

   a quarter   A nickel, . . .

   a peso

4. Guatemala   Guatemala, . . .

   Peru

   Nicaragua   All of these are . . .

   Costa Rica

5. Washington, D.C.   All of these are . . .

   Paris

   Moscow   Washington, . . .

   Rio de Janeiro

Look Back

A. Vocabulary

DIRECTIONS: Circle the letter of the choice that best completes each sentence.

1. Chicken and noodles are two ____ in chicken noodle soup.

   a. mixtures   b. divisions   c. ingredients

2. A group of people with many different religions, languages, and races is a ____ group.

   a. racial   b. cultural   c. diverse

3. He is a complete stranger to me. I don't know anything about his ____.

   a. concept   b. background   c. assistance

4. ____, the party will begin at 8:00 P.M., but I don't believe it.

   a. Typically   b. Supposedly   c. Positively

5. A class is a ____ of students.

   a. group   b. neighborhood   c. reflection

6. I want to buy the apartment building. Then I will be the ____.

   a. neighbor   b. assistant   c. owner

7. I came to this ____ because I wanted to live in a different area.

   a. place   b. mixture   c. division

8. He ____ lives here. He moved out of town last month.

   a. no longer   b. supposedly   c. permanently

9. She is a very ____ person. She goes to church twice a week.

   a. unwilling   b. political   c. religious

10. I like everything about my apartment ____ the cost. It is too expensive.

   a. with   b. except for   c. entirely

B. Matching

DIRECTIONS: *Find the word or phrase in column B which has a similar meaning to a word or phrase in column A. Write the letter of that word or phrase next to the word or phrase in column A.*

	A		B
1. __c__	opportunity	a.	an area of a town or city
2. __j__	varied	b.	have together
3. __g__	except for	c.	chance
4. __f__	entirely	d.	try to find
5. __h__	such as	e.	name
6. __d__	look for	f.	all
7. __a__	neighborhood	g.	but
8. __i__	recent	h.	for example
9. __e__	call	i.	close to the present
10. __b__	share	j.	diverse

chapter 3

Cities in America

A First Look

A. Main Idea

DIRECTIONS: *Before you begin to read, look at these main ideas. There is one main idea for each paragraph. Write the number of the paragraph next to the main idea of that paragraph. Work* very quickly. *Do not read every word.*

1. _____2_____ population information
2. _____7_____ cities are living again   *alive*
3. _____4_____ where people are moving now
4. _____1_____ a description of cities
5. _____3_____ a house in the suburbs
6. _____5_____ a new type of city resident
7. _____6_____ results of the move back to the cities

B. Reading

DIRECTIONS: *Now read carefully.*

1	American cities are similar to other cities around the world: In every country, cities reflect the values of the culture. Cities contain the very best aspects of a society: opportunities for education, employment, and entertainment. They also contain the very worst parts of a society: violent crime, racial conflict, and poverty. American cities are changing, just as American society is changing.
2	After World War II, the population of most large American cities decreased; however, the population in many Sun Belt cities (those of the South and West) increased. Los Angeles and Houston are cities where population increased. These population shifts (the movement of people) to and from the city reflect the changing values of American society.

1
2
3
4
5
6
7
8
9
10
11
12

During this time, in the late 1940s and early 1950s, city res- 13
idents became wealthier, more prosperous. They had more children. 14
They needed more space. They moved out of their apartments in the 15

3   city to buy their own homes. They bought houses in the suburbs, 16
areas near a city where people live. These are areas without many 17
offices or factories. During the 1950s the American "dream" was to 18
have a house in the suburbs. 19

Now things are changing. The children of the people who left 20
the cities in the 1950s are now adults. They, unlike their parents, 21
want to live in the cities. Some continue to move to cities in the Sun 22
Belt. Cities are expanding and the population is increasing in such 23

4   states as Texas, Florida, and California. Others are moving to older, 24
more established cities of the Northeast and Midwest, such as Bos- 25
ton, Baltimore and Chicago. The government, industry, and indi- 26
viduals are restoring old buildings, revitalizing poor neighborhoods, 27
and rebuilding forgotten areas of these cities. 28

Many young professionals, doctors, lawyers, and executives, 29
are moving back into the city. Many are single; others are married, 30
but often without children. They prefer the city to the suburbs be- 31

5   cause their jobs are there; they are afraid of the fuel shortage; or 32
they just enjoy the excitement and opportunities which the city 33
offers. A new class is moving into the cities—a wealthier, more 34
mobile class. 35

This population shift is bringing problems as well as benefits. 36
Countless poor people must leave their apartments in the city be- 37
cause the owners want to sell the buildings or make condominiums, 38

6   apartments which people buy instead of rent. In the 1950s, many 39
poor people did not have enough money to move to the suburbs; now 40
many of these same people do not have enough money to stay in 41
the cities. 42

Only a few years ago, people thought that the older American 43
7   cities were dying. Some city residents now see a bright, new future. 44
Others see only problems and conflicts. One thing is sure: Many 45
dying cities are alive again. 46

Reading Clues

3.1 Look at paragraph 1. The colon (:) is used two times
in this paragraph.
What does the colon do? It
   (a) introduces a false idea.
   -(b) introduces examples.
   (c) introduces a different idea.

Look at page 223 for the answer.

3.2 Find the definition of condominium in the reading.
What is the definition introduced by?
    (a) a period (.)
  −(b) a comma (,)
    (c) a semicolon (;)

Look at page 223 for the answer.

_____

C. Scanning

DIRECTIONS: Write the number of the paragraph where you find the following information.

a. _____ a bright, new future

b. _____ afraid of the fuel shortage

c. _____ racial conflict and poverty

d. _____ the American "dream"

e. _____ apartments which people buy

f. _____ the children of the people who left the city

g. _____ more children

h. _____ older, more established cities

i. _____ cities are alive

j. _____ a new class of city residents

D. Vocabulary

DIRECTIONS: Look at the following pairs of words. Find the word on the left in the reading.
Compare its meaning to the word(s) on the right. Are the words similar or different?
Write _similar_ or _different_ on the line.

contain (2-3)	have	1.	s
aspects (3)	parts	2.	s
opportunities (3)	chances	3.	s
worst (4)	best (3)	4.	d
conflict (5)	problem	5.	s

violent (5)	peaceful	6.	_d_
poverty (5)	wealth	7.	_d_
decreased (8)	increased (9)	8.	_d_
prosperous (14)	wealthy	9.	_s_
space (15)	area	10.	_s_
suburbs (16)	city	11.	_d_
unlike (21)	different from	12.	_s_
expanding (23)	increasing	13.	_s_
prefer (31)	like better	14.	_s_
mobile (35)	movable	15.	_s_
shift (36)	change	16.	_s_
benefits (36)	problems	17.	_d_
rent (39)	buy	18.	_d_
stay (41)	leave	19.	_d_
revitalizing (27)	restoring	20.	_s_

E. Reading Comprehension

DIRECTIONS: Circle the letter of the choice that best completes each sentence.

1. City residents became wealthier and more prosperous ____ World War II.

   a. during   b. after   c. before

2. The population in Baltimore and Chicago probably ____ in the 1950s.

   a. increased   b. decreased   c. stayed the same

3. According to the article, cities are ____.

   a. dying   b. sick   c. alive again

4. The movement of people to and from the city can explain ____.

   a. social changes   b. the best aspects of a society   c. violent crime

5. In the 1950s many city residents wanted to ____.

   a. live in the suburbs   b. revitalize the city   c. live in apartments

6. ____ is an example of one of the best aspects of society.

   a. Crime   b. Education   c. Poverty

7. In paragraph 5 the author gives ____ reasons why people want to live in cities.

   a. two   b. three   c. four

8. After World War II, population in cities decreased because residents ____.

   a. moved to the suburbs   b. became wealthy   c. bought homes

9. ____ residents probably do not see a bright, new future for the city.

   a. New   b. Poor   c. Professional

10. ____ is not in the Sun Belt.

   a. Los Angeles   b. Houston   c. Boston

Look Again

A. Vocabulary

DIRECTIONS: Circle the letter of the choice that best completes each sentence.

1. The problem of divorce has many different ____.

   a. opportunities   b. benefits   c. aspects

2. The United States is a wealthy nation, but there is still ____ here.

   a. space   b. opportunity   c. poverty

3. I don't like living with a roommate. I'm moving ____ my family's house.

   a. back to   b. from   c. out of

4. She is ____ her sister; she is very tall and her sister is very short.

   a. similar to   b. unlike   c. like

5. One benefit of living in this apartment is that it has more ____.

   a. aspects   b. space   c. shifts

6. This box ____ many old books and souvenirs.

   a. reflects   b. explains   c. contains

7. The population of the world ____ daily.

   a. increases   b. inflates   c. decreases

8. Please don't ____ yet. It's still early.

   a. stay   b. leave   c. shift

9. Do you ____ your apartment or is it a condominium?

   a. shift   b. rent   c. buy

10. He has no job; he is looking for ____.

    a. excitement   b. employment   c. entertainment

B. Reading Comprehension

DIRECTIONS: Circle the letter of the choice that best completes each sentence.

1. The author gives ____ examples of the worst parts of a culture.

   a. two   b. three   c. four

2. Many people are now ____ the city.

   a. moving from   b. leaving   c. returning to

3. "Countless poor people must leave their apartments in the city." This is a ___ .

   a. benefit   b. problem   c. positive aspect

4. A few years ago, the cities were ____.

   a. alive   b. dying   c. entertaining

5. The population of most large American cities ____ after World War II.

   a. decreased   b. increased   c. remained the same

6. The author thinks that cities all over the world are ____.

   a. the same   b. similar   c. different

7. In paragraph 1, the author says that some good aspects of cities are schools, ____, and things to do.

   a. values   b. jobs   c. changes

8. The population in Houston and Los Angeles, ____ the population in most other cities, increased after the war.

   a. similar to   b. unlike   c. as well as

9. According to the author, many city residents now have ____ children.

   a. many   b. few   c. a lot of

10. In paragraph 7, the author talks about the ____ of the city.

    a. bright future   b. benefits   c. opportunities

C. Questions

DIRECTIONS: Answer the following questions.

1. What was the American "dream" in the 1950s?

2. According to the author, why do many people want to live in the city now? Why do you think people want to live in the city?

3. What are some positive aspects of city life?

4. What are some positive aspects of suburban life?

5. What is the conflict in many large cities now?

D. Put in Order

DIRECTIONS: *Mark these events in the order that they happened. Number 1 happened first, number 2 happened second, and so on through number 10.*

a. ___3___ They had large families.

b. ___6___ They moved to the suburbs.

c. ___1___ World War II ended.

d. ___5___ They wanted houses of their own.

e. ___2___ City residents became wealthier.

f. ___7___ Their children grew up.

g. ___8___ They wanted to live in the cities.

h. ___10___ They are rebuilding many cities.

i. ___9___ They are returning to the cities.

j. ___4___ They needed more space.

Contact a Point of View

A. Timed Reading

DIRECTIONS: Read the following point of view and answer the questions in four minutes.

Charlotte and Harry Johnson grew up in the city. They were neighbors as children, <u>fell in love</u>, and got married. They live in an apartment in their old neighborhood, on the south side of town. They have two children, both boys. Harry is a bus driver and Charlotte is a <u>waitress</u> at a neighborhood restaurant.

Mr. Harley, their <u>landlord</u>, bought the apartment building back in the 1920s. The building is getting old now, and Mr. Harley wants to sell it and retire. A Mr. Chin wants to buy the building and make <u>condominiums</u>. He <u>offered</u> Mr. Harley $250,000 for the building. Mr. Harley wants to sell, but he's worried about the Johnsons. They're like family. He even knew their families before Harry and Charlotte were born. He knows they don't have the money and can't buy a condominium. He says, "The boys are like my own grandchildren. What can I do?"

Mr. Chin, of Chin Development Corporation, is a very important force in the revitalization of the south side of town. His company rebuilt the old factory area—a forgotten section of town. His work is bringing new residents and business to the south side. The Chin Development Corporation wants to buy an old apartment building from Mr. Harley. Mr. Chin is offering him a good price for the building. Of course, after reconstruction, the value of the building will increase greatly. "These people don't seem to want progress or improvements. We have to bring new, wealthier residents to the city to keep the city alive."

DIRECTIONS: *Read each of the following statements carefully to determine whether each is true, false, or impossible to know. Check the appropriate blank.*

	TRUE	FALSE	IMPOSSIBLE TO KNOW
1. Charlotte and Harry lived in this neighborhood when they were children.	✓		
2. They have two sons.	✓		
3. Charlotte works in the neighborhood.	✓		
4. Mr. Chin is offering two hundred and fifteen thousand dollars for the building.		✓	
5. The Johnsons like Mr. Harley's family.			✓
6. Mr. Harley has no children.			✓
7. Mr. Chin wants to rent the apartments.		✓	
8. He revitalized only the north side of the city.		✓	
9. Mr. Harley bought the building in 1925.			✓
10. After reconstruction, the value of the building will decrease.		✓	

B. Vocabulary

DIRECTIONS: Circle the letter of the word(s) with the same meaning as the italicized word(s).

1. Mr. Harley is the *landlord*.

   a. renter   b. owner   c. custodian

2. The building is *getting* old.

   a. taking   b. shifting   c. becoming

3. He *is worried* about the Johnsons.

   a. doesn't care   b. is concerned   c. knows

4. They're *like* family.

   a. enjoyable   b. similar to   c. likable

5. Mr. Chin is a very important *force* in redevelopment.

   a. power   b. developer   c. buyer

6. His company rebuilt the old factory area—a *forgotten* section of town.

   a. revitalized   b. important   c. abandoned

7. The *value* of the building will increase after reconstruction.

   a. size   b. worth   c. shape

C. Word Forms

DIRECTIONS: Read the following information about verbs. Then decide if the italicized words in the sentences are nouns or verbs.

A *verb* expresses action (*walk, talk*) or relation (*be, seem*) involving other words. Every sentence has a verb.

	NOUN	VERB
1. Political attitudes often *shift* from left to right.		✓
2. In the 1960s there was a sharp *increase* in crime.	✓	
3. What kind of *change* are you talking about?	✓	
4. The population *shift* to the Sun Belt occurred in the 1970s.	✓	

5. At that time population *increased* in the South, but decreased in the North. _____ ✓_____

6. *Progress* in this kind of weather is impossible. ___✓___ _____

7. Mobility means that people *move* from one situation to another. _____ ___✓___

8. The members reported little *progress* in the talks. ___✓___ _____

9. Don't make a *move*! ___✓___ _____

10. It sometimes seems that things *change* slowly. _____ ___✓___

D. Speaking

DIRECTIONS: Complete the following sentences based on the information in the timed reading.

There are two points of view in this reading.
1. Mr. Harley wants to . . .
   Mr. Harley is worried because . . .
2. Mr. Chin wants to . . .
   Mr. Chin thinks that the old neighborhood and its residents . . .

What is your point of view?
Mr. Harley should . . .
Mr. Chin should . . .
Mr. Johnson should . . ,

E. Writing

DIRECTIONS: Go back to the timed reading. Take the part of either Mr. Harley or Mr. Chin. Rewrite paragraph 2 for Mr. Harley. Rewrite paragraph 3 for Mr. Chin.

Begin like this:
    My name is Harley. I am the landlord of an . . .
or like this:
    My name is Chin. I am the owner of the . . .

Look Back

A. Vocabulary

DIRECTIONS: Circle the letter of the choice that best completes each sentence.

1. She is very kind to all the people who live on her street. She is very ____.

   a. neighborly   b. wealthy   c. reflective

2. I live near the city. I take the ____ bus and I get to the office in twenty minutes.

   a. revitalized   b. social   c. suburban

3. Yesterday I found an old table in my grandmother's house. It is old, but with some

   _____ , it will be beautiful.

   a. employment   b. restoration   c. opportunity

4. We do not agree. We can't decide. Our ideas are ____.

   a. entertaining   b. conflicting   c. expanding

5. Condominiums are ____ for some city residents.

   a. mobile   b. rebuilding   c. beneficial

6. You must ____ production to earn money.

   a. decrease   b. contain   c. increase

7. He is a peaceful man. He doesn't like ____.

   a. entertainment   b. violence   c. opportunity

8. That movie is not good for children. It's a(n) ____ movie.

   a. modern   b. prosperous   c. adult

9. That apartment has many large rooms; it's very ____.

   a. residential   b. excitable   c. spacious

10. Poverty and ____ are negative aspects of modern city life.

    a. prosperity   b. violence   c. similarity

B. Matching

DIRECTIONS: Find the word or phrase in column B which has a similar meaning to a word or phrase in column A. Write the letter of that word or phrase next to the word or phrase in column A.

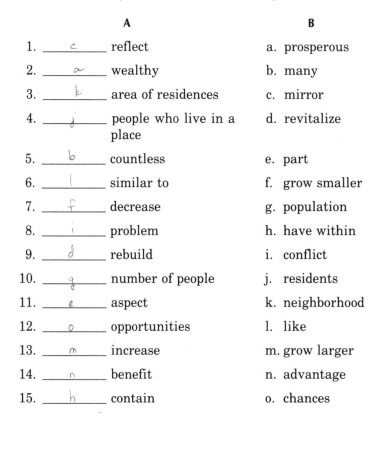

	A		B
1. _c_	reflect	a.	prosperous
2. _a_	wealthy	b.	many
3. _k_	area of residences	c.	mirror
4. _j_	people who live in a place	d.	revitalize
5. _b_	countless	e.	part
6. _l_	similar to	f.	grow smaller
7. _f_	decrease	g.	population
8. _i_	problem	h.	have within
9. _d_	rebuild	i.	conflict
10. _g_	number of people	j.	residents
11. _e_	aspect	k.	neighborhood
12. _o_	opportunities	l.	like
13. _m_	increase	m.	grow larger
14. _n_	benefit	n.	advantage
15. _h_	contain	o.	chances

chapter 4

Food in America

A First Look

A. Main Idea

1. ___4___ fast food

2. ___2___ ethnicity in food

3. ___1___ traditional food in the United States

4. ___3___ a return to natural, unprocessed food

5. ___5___ changing attitudes about food

B. Reading

DIRECTIONS: *Now read carefully.*

1	Many changes are taking place in "food styles" in the United States. The United States is traditionally famous for its very solid and unchanging diet of meat and potatoes. Now we have many different alternatives to choose from: various ethnic food, health food, and fast food, in addition to the traditional home-cooked meal.	*1* *2* *3* *4* *5*
2	Ethnic restaurants and supermarkets are commonplace in the United States. Because the United States is a country of immigrants, there is an immense variety. Any large American city is filled with restaurants serving international cooking. Many cities even have ethnic sections: Chinatown, Little Italy, or Germantown. With this vast ethnic choice, we can enjoy food from all over the world. This is a pleasant thought for those who come here to travel or to work; they can usually find their native specialties: tabouli, arepas, or miso soup. Besides sections of the cities, there are regions which are well known for certain food because of the people who settled there.	*6* *7* *8* *9* *10* *11* *12* *13* *14* *15*

For example, southern California has many Mexican restaurants,   16
and Louisiana has a strong Creole accent to its food. (Creole is a   17
mixture of French, African, and Carribean Island food.)   18

Health food gained popularity when people began to think more   19
seriously about their physical well-being. The very term *health food*   20
is ironic because it implies that there is also "unhealthy" food.   21
Health food includes natural food with minimal processing; i.e.,   22
there are no preservatives to help it last longer or other chem-   23
icals to make it taste or look better. Most health food enthusiasts   24
are vegetarians: They eat no meat; they prefer to get their essential   25
proteins from other sources, such as beans, cheese, and eggs.   26

Fast-food restaurants are now expanding rapidly all over the   27
country. In the United States, speed is a very important factor.   28
People usually have a short lunch break or they just do not want   29
to waste their time eating. Fast-food restaurants are places which   30
take care of hundreds of people in a short time. There is usually   31
very little waiting, and the food is always cheap. Some examples   32
are 'burger and pizza places.   33

America's attitude toward food is changing, too. The traditional   34
big breakfast and dinner at 6:00 P.M. are losing popularity. People   35
are rediscovering the social importance of food. Dinner with family   36
or friends is again becoming a very special way of enjoying and   37
sharing. Like so many people in other cultures, many Americans   38
are taking time to relax and enjoy the finer tastes at dinner, even   39
if they still rush through lunch at a hamburger stand.   40

3

4

5

Reading Clue

4.1   Look at line 22. What does *i.e.* introduce?
       (a) a new idea
       (b) the explanation of an idea
       (c) a contrast (a different idea)
Look at page 223 for the answer.

C. Scanning

DIRECTIONS: Write the number of the paragraph where you find the fol-
lowing information.

a. ___4___ food is always cheap

b. ___2___ Mexican restaurants

c. ___3___ no preservatives

d. ___4___ very little waiting

e. ___2___ Little Italy

f. ___1___ the traditional home-cooked meal

g. ___2___ vast ethnic choice

h. ___2___ native specialties

i. ___4___ speed is important

j. ___1___ different alternatives

D. Vocabulary

DIRECTIONS: *Look at the following pairs of words. Find the word on the left in the reading. Compare its meaning to the words on the right. Are the words similar or different? Write similar or different on the line.*

traditional (5)	new	1. ___d___
famous (2)	well-being	2. ___d___
unchanging (3)	fixed	3. ___s___
alternatives (4)	choices	4. ___s___
various (4)	different	5. ___s___
commonplace (6)	unusual	6. ___d___
ethnic (6, 11)	cultural	7. ___s___
native (13)	foreign	8. ___d___
regions (14)	areas	9. ___s___
gain (19)	lose	10. ___d___
term (20)	expression	11. ___s___
well-being (20)	benefit	12. ___s___
ironic (21)	strange	13. ___s___

minimal (22)	a lot	14. _____ d _____
vegetarian (25)	meat eater	15. _____ d _____
essential (25)	extra	16. _____ d _____
waste (30)	use well	17. _____ d _____
take care of (31)	serve	18. _____ s _____
attitude (34)	feeling	19. _____ s _____
take time (38-39)	rush (40)	20. _____ d _____

E. Reading Comprehension

DIRECTIONS: Circle the letter of the choice that best completes each sentence.

1. Because the United States is a country of immigrants, ____.

   a. food is commonplace
   b. there are many international restaurants
   c. large cities are filled with restaurants

2. One example of health food is a(n) ____.

   a. egg
   b. hamburger
   c. steak

3. Speed is a factor in the increase of ____.

   a. our attitude
   b. lunch breaks
   c. fast-food restaurants

4. Health food enthusiasts usually ____.

   a. like meat
   b. are vegetarian
   c. eat processed food

5. People who come to the United States should not be homesick because ____.

   a. they can find their native food
   b. there are many regional specialties
   c. American food is traditional

6. Germantown is an example of ____.

   a. international cooking
   b. an ethnic neighborhood
   c. a regional specialty

7. The author thinks that Americans are now eating dinner ____.

   a. at 6:00 P.M.
   b. more quickly
   c. later

8. Meat and potatoes are examples of ____.

   a. the traditional American diet
   b. processed food
   c. health

9. The author speaks about ____ different types of food, in addition to traditional food.

   a. two   b. three   c. four

10. Americans are relaxing at dinner, but they are still ____ .

   a. rushing at lunch   b. sharing it   c. losing popularity

Look Again

A. Vocabulary

DIRECTIONS: Circle the letter of the choice that best completes each sentence.

1. She is always on television. She is a(n) ____ newscaster.

   a. traditional   b. essential   c. well-known

2. Fast-food restaurants are now ____ .

   a. specialties   b. commonplace   c. factors

✱ 3. Immigration is the most important factor in the ____ of ethnic restaurants.

   a. sharing   b. source   c. well-being

4. It is ____ that they call her *Smiley*; I never see her smile.

   a. ironic   b. alternative   c. various

5. It is ____ to have protein.

   a. traditional   b. ethnic   c. essential

6. Many people ____ energy; they use it without thinking.

   a. waste   b. rush   c. rediscover

7. *Fast food* ____ speed.

   a. contains   b. implies   c. takes care of

8. There is ____ interest in Italian food in the Japanese section of town.

   a. immense   b. pleasant   c. minimal

9. Meat is a ____ of protein.

   a. factor   b. taste   c. source

10. American Indians are ____ Americans.

   a. native   b. foreign   c. international

B. Reading Comprehension

DIRECTIONS: Circle the letter of the choice that best completes each sentence.

1. According to the author, the ____ is *not* changing very much.

   a. early dinner   b. fast lunch   c. big breakfast

2. The last sentence of the article means that Americans are changing ____ of their attitudes.

   a. some   b. all   c. none

3. The author says that fast food is popular at lunch because people don't have time or they don't want to ____ .

   a. spend much money   b. eat hamburgers   c. have a short lunch break

4. An example of the traditional American attitude toward food is ____ .

   a. a late dinner   b. a quick lunch   c. health food

5. ____ is a source of protein.

   a. Fruit   b. Meat   c. Natural food

6. The author gives ____ examples of regional specialties.

   a. four   b. three   c. two

7. In the last sentence, the author says that people in other cultures ____ .

   a. rush through lunch   b. relax at dinner   c. are socially important

8. Preservatives make frozen food ____ .

   a. taste better   b. last longer   c. look better

9. Fast-food restaurants usually serve ____ .

   a. health food   b. hamburger specialties   c. ethnic food

10. Two important factors in fast-food restaurants are ____ .

    a. speed and cost   b. expansion and lunch breaks   c. 'burger and pizza places

C. Questions

DIRECTIONS: Answer the following questions.

1. Are there fast-food restaurants in your country? What is the attitude of the citizens toward them? Are they popular?

2. What do you consider typical American cooking?

3. Why is it difficult to define American cooking?

4. What surprised you most about American food?

5. Can you find most food from your native land in the United States? What food can you not find?

6. What aspect of America's attitude toward food would you like to change? Why?

Contact a Point of View

A. Timed Reading

DIRECTIONS: Read the following point of view and answer the questions in four minutes.

All right! Enough cookies, cola, and chips! It seems that junk food is all that the children want to eat these days. Television controls their tastes. The kids see well-known personalities eating potato chips, candy, and other processed food, and they want to be like their heroes. How do they do it? They eat the same food. I wish there were more characters like old Popeye the sailor, who ate spinach and not french fries.

Now I don't expect my children to eat health food because I like brown rice, beans, and fresh vegetables. I'm glad to cook traditional meals of meat and potatoes for them. I really can't be too upset with the kids because most adults aren't careful about what they eat. The other night, my wife and I went to a party where there was plenty to drink but very little for us to eat. They served hotdogs and hamburgers. I can't eat hotdogs, with all those preservatives, and hamburgers are filled with chemicals so that they look better. Besides the meat, they had sugar-filled cookies and cake, and, of course, chips. Terrible! I don't want the world to change because of me, but I think that people should realize that there are alternatives to eating meat. They always tell me that I probably don't get my essential proteins. I feel better than ever and I'm sure that it's because I'm a vegetarian. I would really like to see more television advertisements which show the benefits of good, healthy, natural food.

DIRECTIONS: Read each of the following statements carefully to determine whether each is true, false, or impossible to know. Check the appropriate blank.

	TRUE	FALSE	IMPOSSIBLE TO KNOW
1. Cookies and chips are junk food.	✓		
2. The author feels very healthy.	✓		
3. Brown rice is junk food.		✓	
4. Children want to eat junk food.	✓		
5. The author eats meat.		✓	
6. The author is married.	✓		
7. Television influences children's food choice.	✓		
8. Popeye ate only junk food.		✓	
9. There are many TV advertisements for health food.			✓
10. If necessary, the author will serve meat and potatoes to the kids.	✓		

B. Vocabulary

DIRECTIONS: *Fill in the blanks in the sentences with vocabulary from the reading. Make necessary changes in the form of the word.*

1. processed/junk/taste/spinach

   _____is not _____food; it _____good because it is not _____ or treated with chemicals.

2. essential/careful/enough/plenty

   People should be _____about getting _____ of _____proteins. Many people do not get _____ .

3. fresh/expect/upset

   She was _____ at the restaurant because she _____to get _____vegetables, not canned ones.

4. personalities/heroes/control

   Many children's_____are TV_____.
   These people often _____the attitudes of the children.

C. Word Forms

DIRECTIONS: *Look at the endings for <u>adjectives</u> below. Are the italicized words in the sentences adjectives or nouns?*

NOUNS	ADJECTIVES
success	success*ful* (full of)
value	value*less* (without)
religion	religi*ous*

Note that *-ful* and *-less* cannot be added to all nouns. For example, "valueful" is not a word, but valueless is.

	NOUN	ADJECTIVE
1. His work is always *careless* and messy.	_____	✓
2. That's a *wonderful* idea.	_____	✓

	NOUN	ADJECTIVE
3. A *thoughtful* person is one who is kind.	_____	___✓___
4. There are *various* possibilities for the party.	_____	___✓___
5. Everyone was shocked. It was a *senseless* murder.	_____	___✓___
6. He does everything with *care*.	___✓___	_____
7. What price is *success*?	___✓___	_____
8. Only a few things in life are *changeless*.	_____	___✓___
9. That diamond is a *priceless* antique.	_____	___✓___
10. She watched the kitten with *wonder*.	___✓___	_____

D. Speaking

DIRECTIONS: America's attitude toward food is different from many other countries. Have you changed your "food style" in the United
States? Put a check beside the following statements that are
true for you. Share your ideas with a classmate or with the
class.

In the United States, I eat

_____ a bigger breakfast

_____ a faster lunch

_____ an earlier lunch

_____ a smaller lunch

_____ more

_____ less

_____ more meat

_____ less meat

_____ more junk food

_____ dinner earlier

_____ more sweets

_____ more frozen food

_____ more at parties

_____ in restaurants more often

_____ more canned food

_____ more fresh food

In the United States, I ate some things for the first time.

I really like _____.

I really hate _____.

E. Writing

DIRECTIONS: Write a short composition about food. Compare the food style in your country with that in the United States. Use the vocabulary from exercise D.

Example: People in my country eat a smaller breakfast than people in the United States. They eat . . .

Look Back

A. Vocabulary

DIRECTIONS: Circle the letter of the choice that best completes each sentence.

1. He is a strong, ____ candidate for the presidency.

   a. commonplace   b. solid   c. rushed

2. Using a lot of electricity is ____.

   a. rediscovering   b. wasteful   c. well known

3. The Pacific Ocean is very ____.

   a. processed   b. expansive   c. gaining

4. The food is inexpensive but ____.

   a. tasty   b. social   c. structured

5. He dislikes everything; he has a very poor ____.

   a. well-being   b. popularity   c. attitude

6. There are ____ immigrant groups in most large American cities.

   a. various   b. unchanging   c. popular

7. What kind of ____ does that pie have?

   a. filling   b. importance   c. pleasantness

8. ____ is important in fish.

   a. Control   b. Freshness   c. Diet

9. ____ is an important factor for most movie personalities.

   a. Fame   b. Gain   c. Irony

10. The ____ of life is a question for all human beings. What is life's meaning?

    a. waste   b. essence   c. attitude

B. Matching

DIRECTIONS: *Find the word in column B which has a similar meaning to a word in column A. Write the letter of that word next to the word in column A.*

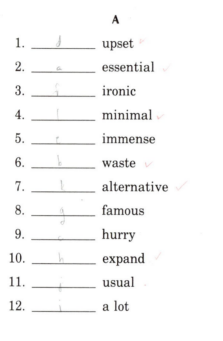

	A		B
1. ___d___	upset	a.	necessary
2. ___a___	essential	b.	use poorly
3. ___f___	ironic	c.	rush
4. ___l___	minimal	d.	worried
5. ___e___	immense	e.	large
6. ___b___	waste	f.	strange
7. ___k___	alternative	g.	well known
8. ___g___	famous	h.	grow
9. ___c___	hurry	i.	plenty
10. ___h___	expand	j.	commonplace
11. ___j___	usual	k.	choice
12. ___i___	a lot	l.	almost none

Culture Shock

A First Look

A. Main Idea

DIRECTIONS: *Before you begin to read, look at these main ideas. There is one main idea for each paragraph in the reading. Write the number of the paragraph next to the main idea of that paragraph. Work <u>very quickly</u>. Do not read every word at this point.*

1. _____ the people who experience culture shock

2. _____ the things people say when you leave home

3. _____ three stages of culture shock

4. _____ the feelings of culture shock

5. _____ problems in a new culture

6. _____ definition of culture shock

B. Reading

DIRECTIONS: *Now read carefully.*

1   "You're going to the United States to live? How wonderful!   *1*
You're really lucky!"   *2*
      Does this sound familiar? Perhaps your family and friends said   *3*
similar things to you when you left home. But does it seem true all   *4*
the time? Is your life in this new country always wonderful and   *5*
2   exciting? Specialists in counseling and intercultural studies say that   *6*
it is not easy to adjust to life in a new culture. They call the feelings   *7*
which people experience when they come to a new environment   *8*
culture shock.   *9*
      According to these specialists, there are three stages of culture   *10*
shock. In the first stage, the newcomers like their environment.   *11*
Then, when the newness wears off, they begin to hate the city, the   *12*
3   country, the people, the apartment, and everything else in the new   *13*
culture. In the final stage of culture shock, the newcomers begin to   *14*
adjust to their surroundings and, as a result, enjoy their life more.   *15*
      Some of the factors in culture shock are obvious. Maybe the   *16*

weather is unpleasant. Perhaps the customs are different. Perhaps 17
the public service systems such as the telephone, post office, or 18
transportation are difficult to figure out and you make mistakes. 19
The simplest things seem difficult. The language may be difficult. 20
How many times have you just repeated the same thing again and 21
again and hoped to understand the answer eventually? The food 22
may seem strange to you and you may miss the familiar smells of 23
the food you are accustomed to in your own country. If you don't 24
look similar to the natives, you may feel strange. You may feel like 25
everyone is watching you. In fact, you are always watching yourself. 26
You are self-conscious. 27

4

Who experiences culture shock? Everyone does in some form 28
or another. But culture shock comes as a surprise to most people. 29
A lot of the time, the people with the worst culture shock are the 30
people who never had any difficulties in their own countries. They 31
were active and successful in their community. They had hobbies 32
or pastimes which they enjoyed. When they come to a new country, 33
they do not have the same established positions or hobbies. They 34
find themselves without a role, almost without an identity. They 35
have to build a new self-image. 36

5

Culture shock produces a feeling of disorientation. This dis- 37
orientation may be homesickness, imagined illnesses, or even para- 38
noia (unreasonable fear). When people feel the disorientation of 39
culture shock, they sometimes feel like staying inside all the time. 40
They want to protect themselves from the unfamiliar environment. 41
They want to create an escape within their room or apartment to 42
give themselves a sense of security. This escape does solve the prob- 43
lem of culture shock for the short term, but it does nothing to fa- 44
miliarize the person more with the culture. Familiarity and expe- 45
rience are the long-term solutions to the problem of culture shock. 46

6

Reading Clue

5.1 Find three words in paragraph 3 that introduce a
sequence or progression. What are these words?
Look at page 223 for the answer.

C. Scanning

*DIRECTIONS: Write the number of the paragraph where you find the fol-
lowing information.*

a. _____ feelings which people experience

b. _____ difficult language

c. _____ paranoia

d. _____ a new self-image

e. _____ disorientation

f. _____ you're lucky

g. _____ public service systems

h. _____ stages of culture shock

i. _____ homesickness

j. _____ for the short term

D. Vocabulary

DIRECTIONS: *Look at the following pairs of words. Find the word on the left in the reading. Compare its meaning to the word(s) on the right. Are the word(s) similar or different? Write* similar *or* different *on the line.*

lucky (2)	unlucky	1.	d
intercultural (6)	between cultures	2.	s
environment (8)	surroundings (15)	3.	s
hate (12)	love	4.	d
stage (10, 14)	progressive part	5.	s
newcomer (14)	natives (25)	6.	d
final (14)	last	7.	s
obvious (16)	easy to see	8.	s
customs (17)	transportation	9.	d
figure out (19)	understand	10.	s
simplest (20)	most difficult	11.	d
strange (23)	odd	12.	s
miss (23)	forget	13.	d
the worst (30)	the best	14.	d
disorientation (37)	strangeness	15.	s

imagined (38)	real	16. _____ d _____
illness (38)	sickness	17. _____ s _____
unfamiliar (41)	familiar	18. _____ d _____
term (44, 46)	length of time	19. _____ s _____
solution (46)	problem	20. _____ d _____

E. Reading Comprehension

DIRECTIONS: Circle the letter of the choice that best completes each sentence.

1. There are apparently ____ stages of culture shock.

   a. two   b. three   c. four

2. People who come to a new environment ____ feel lucky and happy.

   a. do not always   b. always   c. never

3. According to the author, it ____ easy to adjust to a new culture.

   a. is always   b. is usually   c. is not

✻ 4. The author gives ____ examples of public service systems.

   a. two   b. three   c. four

5. Someone who looks ____ the natives of a country may feel strange.

   a. similar to   b. at   c. different from

6. People in a foreign culture feel ____ about themselves and their positions.

   a. differently   b. the same   c. happy

✻ 7. The author gives ____ examples of the disorientation of culture shock.

   a. two   b. three   c. four

8. The author thinks that it is ____ idea for people feeling culture shock to stay in their homes as a long-term solution to culture shock.

   a. not a good   b. a great   c. not a bad

9. In the final stage of culture shock, people ____ the new environment.

   a. love   b. adjust to   c. hate

10. People who feel culture shock stay at home because of ____ .

   a. insecurity   b. solutions   c. the weather

Look Again

A. Vocabulary

DIRECTIONS: Circle the letter of the choice that best completes each sentence.

1. In this reading, a specialist is probably ____ .

   a. a doctor   b. an authority   c. a newcomer

2. Your ____ is the area around you.

   a. environment   b. culture   c. self-image

3. Disorientation is a feeling of ____ .

   a. security   b. knowledge   c. unreality

4. I can't figure out my homework. I can't ____ it.

   a. remember   b. escape from   c. understand

5. I am bored. My life is not ____ enough.

   a. experienced   b. active   c. essential

6. People usually have hobbies for ____ .

   a. money   b. enjoyment   c. a job

7. A newcomer is ____ with the area around him or her.

   a. unfamiliar   b. unhappy   c. accustomed to

8. When you feel that everyone is watching you, you are ____ .

   a. secure   b. self-conscious   c. unfamiliar

9. Paranoia is a feeling of ____ .

   a. fear   b. happiness   c. experience

10. I don't know him. I don't know his ____ .

    a. system   b. identity   c. term

B. Reading Comprehension

DIRECTIONS: Circle the letter of the choice that best completes each sentence.

1. Adjustment to a new culture is the _____ stage of culture shock.

    a. first   b. second   c. final

2. It is _____ for a newcomer to hate the new environment at some time in the adjustment to the new surroundings.

    a. strange   b. entertaining   c. typical

3. According to the author, adjustment to a new culture is _____ .

    a. difficult   b. easy   c. familiar

4. Simple things are _____ difficult in a new culture.

    a. never   b. sometimes   c. not

5. Systems for public services are _____ all over the world.

    a. different   b. the same   c. simple

6. Culture shock _____ affects people who were successful and active in their own countries.

    a. often   b. never   c. always

7. When people feel culture shock, they may feel _____ .

    a. fear   b. happiness   c. familiar

8. People in culture shock who stay at home solve their problems _____ .

    a. forever   b. for a long time   c. for a short time

9. When people come to a new country, they do not usually have _____ .

    a. culture shock   b. established positions   c. public service

10. The author thinks that people _____ their hobbies in their own country.

    a. do not enjoy   b. leave   c. never have

C. Questions

DIRECTIONS: Answer the following questions.

1. What happens in the first stage of culture shock?

2. What happens in the second stage of culture shock?

3. What happens in the last stage of culture shock?

4. What are three examples of public service systems?

5. What are three examples of the disorientation of culture shock?

section 3

Contact a Point of View

A. Timed Reading

DIRECTIONS: Read the following point of view and answer the questions in four minutes.

Nguyen Chau Van Loc came to the United States in 1979 from Vietnam. His first impression of the United States was very positive. He was particularly impressed with the way Americans had put technology to work for them. Americans made machines to take them upstairs and downstairs, give them money at the bank, and even open doors for them. He felt that this new environment offered him many exciting opportunities.

However, Nguyen quickly found himself unprepared to take advantage of these opportunities. He knew almost no English. Even when he knew what to say on a bus or in a store, no one understood him and he had to repeat and repeat. In Vietnam, Nguyen was a technician, but in the United States he did not have enough experience compared with other people. He had trouble finding a job. He felt that he did not have an important role or position in the city and missed the security and friendliness of his town in Vietnam. He felt that he would never learn English or feel happy in the United States. He began to feel very depressed and homesick.

Nguyen was lucky because there was a counselor in his English program. This counselor helped Nguyen to understand that his feelings were normal and that they were only a stage in his adjustment to this new culture. Nguyen began to look around him and to talk to other Vietnamese. He saw that many others felt the same way he did. Some, in fact, were more disoriented than he was and were afraid to go out into the city.

Eventually, Nguyen began to feel better about his life in the United States. He developed a position in the Vietnamese American community and adjusted to his new role in American society. He is accustomed to his life in this new country but will always miss Vietnam.

DIRECTIONS: *Read each of the following statements carefully to determine whether each is true, false, or impossible to know. Check the appropriate blank.*

	TRUE	FALSE	IMPOSSIBLE TO KNOW
1. Nguyen came from Vietnam.	✓		
2. Nguyen is married.			✓
3. Nguyen came to the United States in 1977.		✓	
4. Nguyen had a positive attitude about American technology.	✓		
5. Nguyen did not have a job in Vietnam.		✓	
6. A counselor helped Nguyen.	✓		
7. The counselor was a woman.			✓
8. No one felt the same way that Nguyen did.		✓	
9. People understood Nguyen's English easily.		✓	

	TRUE	FALSE	IMPOSSIBLE TO KNOW
10. Nguyen never thinks about Vietnam now.	_____	✓_____	_____

B. Vocabulary

DIRECTIONS: Circle the letter of the word(s) with the same meaning as the italicized word(s).

1. My first *impression of* the teacher was good.

   a. experience with   b. conversation with   c. ideas about

2. American *technology* surprised the Vietnamese immigrant.

   a. scientific development   b. machines   c. industry

3. There are many *opportunities* for work in the city.

   a. possibilities   b. difficulties   c. advantages

4. I wrote my homework *again*.

   a. very well   b. another time   c. finally

5. He felt *self-conscious* when he spoke English.

   a. strong   b. tired   c. insecure

6. He was not sure of his *role* in the group.

   a. position   b. friend   c. pay

7. I am always *depressed* on rainy days.

   a. angry   b. tired   c. sad

8. The *counselor* talked to me about my problems.

   a. assistant   b. advisor   c. teacher

9. The newcomers felt *disoriented* in the airport.

   a. mixed up   b. happy   c. homesick

10. The *image* on this television is bad.

   a. picture   b. actor   c. color

C. Word Forms

DIRECTIONS: Look at the endings for nouns and adjectives below. Are the italicized words in the sentences nouns or adjectives? Remember that there is never an s on the ends of adjectives in English.

	NOUN	ADJECTIVE
society	*social*	
tradition	*traditional*	

	NOUN	ADJECTIVE
1. This solution will be *beneficial* for everyone.	_____	_____
2. Our sense of *community* is very important.	_____	_____
3. *Poverty* is a serious social problem.	_____	_____
4. *Racial* conflict is an issue in the United States.	_____	_____
5. She is always very *practical*.	_____	_____
6. Downtown is the *central* business area.	_____	_____
7. What is a *typical* name in your country?	_____	_____
8. There is some *similarity* between you and your brother.	_____	_____
9. Who has *control* here?	_____	_____
10. People in certain countries value *formality* greatly.	_____	_____

D. Speaking

DIRECTIONS: When you entered a new environment or culture, what was the most difficult thing you experienced? What was the easiest? Number these things according to the level of difficulty. Write 1 for the hardest and 10 for the easiest. Include all the numbers from 1 to 10.

_____ the bank

_____ the transportation system

_____ the post office

_____ the living situation (roommates, finding a place to live, neighbors)

_____ making friends

_____ the weather

_____ understanding American customs and lifestyles

_____ understanding American values and beliefs

_____ using the telephone

_____ finding good food to eat

Explain to the other people in your class why you had difficulties with your number 1, the hardest thing. Give examples of your experiences. After you were in this new environment for a while or even now, what was or is the most difficult thing for you? Did the most difficult thing become easier in time or did it stay the same?

E. Writing

DIRECTIONS: *(1) Put the verb in parentheses () in the past tense.*
(2) Put the sentences in order (1, 2, 3 . . .).
(3) Write all the sentences in a paragraph.

_____ Even when he (know) _____ what to say, nobody

(understand) _____ him.

_____ His first impression of the United States (be) _____ very
positive.

_____ However, Nguyen quickly (find) _____ himself unprepared to take advantage of these opportunities.

___*1*___ Nguyen Chau Van Loc (come) ___*came*___ to the United States
in 1979 from Vietnam.

_____ Eventually, Nguyen (begin) _____ to feel better about
his life in the United States.

_____ He (feel) _____ that this modern country (offer)

_____ him many opportunities.

_____ This was because he (know) _____ almost no English.

_____ However, he knows that he will always miss Vietnam.

Look Back

A. Vocabulary

DIRECTIONS: Circle the letter of the choice that best completes each sentence.

1. The man studied in the field for thirty-five years. He is a ____ in the field.

   a. counselor   b. newcomer   c. specialist

2. I was certainly surprised when I heard the news. I was ____ .

   a. shocked   b. bored   c. accustomed to it

3. Childhood is the first ____ of a person's life. Or is it the second?

   a. stage   b. image   c. impression

4. I collect stamps. That is my ____ .

   a. development   b. hobby   c. source

5. My first ____ of the airport was terrible.

   a. impression   b. newness   c. alternative

6. Some medicine makes people feel tired and ____ .

   a. homesick   b. familiar   c. disoriented

7. He was born in Kentucky. He is a ____ of Kentucky.

   a. native   b. newcomer   c. term

8. There is a good ____ feeling in our neighborhood. We all help each other.

   a. custom   b. self-conscious   c. community

9. I have to find a ____ for this problem.

   a. stage   b. custom   c. solution

10. He imagined that people were trying to kill him. He was very ____ .

   a. successful   b. paranoid   c. established

B. Matching

DIRECTIONS: Find the word or phrase in column B which has a similar meaning to a word in column A. Write the letter of that word or phrase next to the word in column A.

	A		B
1.	_j_ image	a.	say again
2.	_f_ unfamiliar	b.	assistance
3.	_a_ repeat	c.	easy
4.	_b_ service	d.	change a little
5.	_g_ fear	e.	stranger
6.	_i_ environment	f.	strange
7.	_e_ newcomer	g.	fright
8.	_d_ adjust	h.	very sad
9.	_c_ simple	i.	area around you
10.	_h_ depressed	j.	picture

Contemporary American Society

A First Look

A. Main Idea

DIRECTIONS: *Before you begin to read, look at these main ideas. There is one main idea for each paragraph. Write the number of the paragraph next to the main idea of that paragraph. Work <u>very quickly</u>. Do not read every word at this point.*

1. _____ a transient society

2. _____ marriage and divorce

3. _____ readjustment after divorce

4. _____ traditional life in a small town

B. Reading

DIRECTIONS: *Now read carefully.*

1

    In the past fifty years, American society has changed a great   1
deal. Fifty years ago, most Americans lived in small communities.   2
They rarely moved from one area to another and knew their neigh-   3
bors at least by name if not by close, personal interaction. Life was   4
so personal in those days that people often joked about it. They said   5
that a person could not even stay home from church on Sunday   6
without the whole town knowing about it. It was difficult to have   7
privacy in a small community like that, but there was usually a   8
sense of security, of belonging, and of community togetherness in   9
such places. Except for church and the local movie theater, there   10
was not much in the way of entertainment. Some people dreamed   11
about moving to the exciting life of the big cities, but most people   12
were happy to live all their lives in the same community.   13
    Few people experience this type of lifelong social interaction   14
or sense of community togetherness now. Contemporary American   15
society is much more transient now; people often move from neigh-   16

borhood to neighborhood, city to city, and coast to coast. It is rare   17
to find people who have lived all their lives in one community.   18
Because people move so frequently, they do not have a chance to   19
get to know their neighbors. Perhaps this is also why Americans   20
tend to have a more casual attitude about friendships than people   21
from some other cultures; Americans are accustomed to leaving   22
friends and making new friends. This transience contributes to a   23
sense of being part of a very impersonal society in which people   24
have lost the habit of saying hello to people they pass on the streets   25
or in the hallways of their apartment buildings.   26

The American family has also gone through many changes in   27
the past fifty years. Primary among these changes is the current   28
attitude about divorce, the legal end of a marriage. Sociologists   29
predict that 40 percent of all marriages in the United States in the   30
1980s will end in divorce. However, this is a partially misleading   31
statement—four out of five of all divorced people marry again. Mar-   32
riage and family are still very important to Americans, in spite of   33
the divorce statistics. With less emphasis on tradition, on religion,   34
and on the economic dependence of women on men (due to the in-   35
crease of women who work), Americans seem less likely to remain   36
in a marriage that has problems. They are not forced by economic,   37
social, or religious pressure to stay married. Partly as a reaction to   38
the high divorce rate, many American young people live together   39
without being married. They feel that it is a good idea to know each   40
other well before they become legally tied. This is particularly com-   41
mon in the more liberal areas of the country—the East and West   42
Coasts and the large cities of the North.   43

Nowadays, single-parent families, even if temporary, are in-   44
creasingly common. After a divorce, parents and children must es-   45
tablish new types of relationships. These relationships depend on   46
who has custody of the children and how often the other parent sees   47
the children. The establishment of new relationships is also a focus   48
of families when divorced parents remarry and bring children from   49
their previous marriage to live with a new parent and, perhaps,   50
with that person's children. These children sometimes have more   51
stepparents, stepbrothers and sisters, and stepgrandparents than   52
they know what to do with. This can, of course, have both negative   53
and positive effects on the children, depending on the personalities   54
of the people involved. When these children grow up, it will be   55
interesting to see how they in turn deal with family life and society   56
in the United States.   57

Reading Clues

6.1 Find the words *rarely* (line 3), *few* (line 14), and *rare* (line 12). These words are ____ .
   (a) affirmative
   (b) negative
Look at page 223 for the answer.

6.2 Find a word in both line 7 and line 40 which shows negation.
         What is this word?
Look at page 224 for the answer.

C. Scanning

DIRECTIONS: *Write the number of the paragraph where you find the following information.*

a. _____ local movie theater

b. _____ stepparents

c. _____ divorce statistics

d. _____ more liberal areas of the country

e. _____ legally tied

f. _____ making new friends

g. _____ a sense of belonging

h. _____ coast to coast

i. _____ the hallways of apartment buildings

j. _____ from their previous marriage

D. Vocabulary

DIRECTIONS: *Look at the following pairs of words. Find the word on the left in the reading. Compare its meaning to the word(s) on the right. Are the words similar or different? Write* similar *or* different *on the line.*

rarely (3)	often	1. _____ d _____
personal (4)	impersonal (24)	2. _____ d _____
interaction (4, 14)	person-to-person contact	3. _____ s _____
togetherness (9)	closeness	4. _____ s _____
contemporary (15)	modern	5. _____ s _____
transient (16)	permanent	6. _____ d _____
coast (17)	inland	7. _____ d _____
rare (17)	common	8. _____ d _____
casual (21)	formal	9. _____ d _____
contributes (23)	adds	10. _____ s _____
current (28)	old	11. _____ d _____
predict (30)	talk about the past	12. _____ d _____
pressure (38)	force	13. _____ s _____
legally tied (41)	married	14. _____ s _____
common (41)	unusual	15. _____ d _____
liberal (42)	conservative	16. _____ d _____
single (44)	one	17. _____ s _____
establish (45–46)	make	18. _____ s _____
custody (47)	care	19. _____ s _____
deal with (56)	manage	20. _____ s _____

E. Reading Comprehension

DIRECTIONS: Circle the letter of the choice that best completes each sentence.

1. According to the author, life in small communities was _____.

   a. exciting   b. personal   c. private

2. The author states that more women work outside the home now in _____.

   a. single-parent families   b. general   c. two-parent families

3. Single-parent families are ____.

   a. always single-parent families
   b. more common now than before
   c. larger now

4. The author mentions new relationships ____.

   a. with parents and stepfamilies
   b. with one parent only
   c. in remarriage

5. People probably ____ went to church when they lived in small communities.

   a. rarely
   b. often
   c. sometimes

6. People today ____ live all their lives in one community in the United States.

   a. almost never
   b. usually
   c. almost always

7. The author thinks that Americans and people from other cultures have ____ ideas about friendships.

   a. similar
   b. strange
   c. different

8. In paragraph 3, the author mentions ____ things that used to make divorce difficult.

   a. three
   b. four
   c. seven

9. According to the author, people who live together without being married ____ get married in the future.

   a. do not want to
   b. may decide to
   c. usually

10. The author thinks that new relationships with stepfamilies are ____ difficult.

   a. always
   b. sometimes
   c. not

Look Again

A. Vocabulary

DIRECTIONS: Circle the letter of the choice that best completes each sentence.

1. People come and go here all the time. It is really a very ____ community.

   a. misleading   b. transient   c. dependent

2. I never have coffee ____ sugar.

   a. unless   b. in spite of   c. without

3. Business letters are usually very ____.

   a. private   b. impersonal   c. pressured

4. A large salary generally gives people financial ____.

   a. security   b. statistics   c. assistance

5. He was unable to come to the party ____ illness.

   a. because of   b. at least with   c. in spite of

6. I don't know them very well. We are just ____ friends.

   a. personal   b. casual   c. temporary

7. I went swimming ____ the cold water.

   a. depending on   b. in spite of   c. at least in

8. A ____ is something I do without thinking. I am accustomed to it.

   a. tradition   b. habit   c. reaction

9. They did not associate with each other. They had little ____.

   a. dependence   b. personality   c. interaction

10. My father paid for my education. I ____ him for financial support.

    a. depended on   b. established   c. was accustomed to

B. Reading Comprehension

DIRECTIONS: *Circle the letter of the choice that best completes each sentence.*

1. In small communities, people usually knew ____ .

   a. a lot of people fairly well   b. few people   c. close interaction

2. Fifty years ago, Americans moved around ____ .

   a. a lot   b. from one area to another   c. less than they do now

3. The author thinks that a major factor contributing to the impersonality of contemporary society is ____ .

   a. large cities   b. transience   c. apartment buildings

4. ____ percent of divorced people marry again.

   a. Forty   b. Sixty   c. Eighty ⁴⁄₅

5. According to the author, divorce was less common when ____ .

   a. divorce statistics were higher   b. family was more important   c. married women did not work

6. The high divorce rate is ____ why many Americans live together who are not married to each other.

   a. the reason   b. one reason   c. not a reason

7. The author says that there is a sense of security and togetherness but little ____ in small communities.

   a. belonging   b. privacy   c. church

8. The custody of children and frequency of visits to a divorced parent are ____ .

   a. fixed   b. variable   c. laws

9. The author thinks that ____ is a difficult part of contemporary family life.

   a. reestablishing relationships   b. loneliness   c. impersonality

10. The author talks about two major changes in society: changes in the family related to marriage and changes in ____ .

   a. people who live together without being married   b. personal interaction   c. cities

C. Questions

DIRECTIONS: Answer the following questions.

1. What is the major difference between life in small communities fifty years ago and life in the United States now?

2. Why does the author think that Americans have a casual attitude toward friendship in comparison to people from other cultures?

3. What are forces which prevent divorce from being common?

4. Where is it common for young people to live together without being married?

5. What are two examples of changes in the American family structure?

Contact a Point of View

A. Timed Reading

DIRECTIONS: Read the following point of view and answer the questions in four minutes.

My name is Ron Perotta. I have three teenagers, two girls and a boy. I want to tell you it's not easy to have kids nowadays. They all laugh because I'm always saying, "When I was a kid . . . ." But, it's true; when I was a kid, things were different. Families were closer. We all went to church together. I make my family go to church every Sunday, but we are the only ones in our neighborhood who go. So my kids think that religion is just another one of Dad's traditional ideas. There is not much support for traditional ideas nowadays.

It's hard to be a parent these days. My parents never had to worry about drugs, about sex, about the danger for their kids on the street. Kids weren't even supposed to know about sex, unless they lived on a farm, until they were sixteen or so. There were some problems, I guess, even then, but there weren't as many. Drugs and violence weren't all around us like they are now.

Well, I'm a realist. I expect my kids will probably try marijuana and my girls may live with their boyfriends. I won't like it and I'll fight to prevent it, but that's the way it is. But I think that basically my kids are good kids. I think they'll grow up and get married. They'll probably have the same kinds of values that my wife and I have. I just wish it were 1958 again. Those were the good old days!

DIRECTIONS: *Read each of the following statements carefully to determine whether each is true, false, or impossible to know. Check the appropriate blank.*

	TRUE	FALSE	IMPOSSIBLE TO KNOW
1. The writer is a mother.		✓	
2. Ron has six children.		✓	
3. Ron's neighbors go to church every Sunday.		✓	
4. Drugs, sex, and violence were big problems when Ron was young.		✓	
5. Kids who lived on a farm were supposed to know about sex.	✓		
6. Ron thinks it is a good idea for people to live together without being married.		✓	
7. Ron thinks that traditional ideas are unpopular now.	✓		
8. Ron's children tried marijuana last year.			✓
9. Ron thinks that religion is important.	✓		
10. Ron is married.	✓		

B. Vocabulary

DIRECTIONS: Circle the letter of the word(s) with the same meaning as the italicized word(s).

1. We have five *kids*.

   a. parents   b. relatives   c. children

2. It's *hard* to be a parent.

   a. difficult   b. single   c. busy

3. I can't *prevent* my friend from moving.

   a. stop   b. follow   c. develop

4. I am *worried* about my children.

   a. angry   b. concerned   c. idealistic

5. What *kind* of ice cream do you have?

   a. product   b. area   c. type

6. The PTA is the *Parent*-Teacher Association.

   a. child   b. father or mother   c. president

7. They seem to *grow up* too quickly.

   a. become adults   b. take drugs   c. continue

8. In *those days* I felt like a different person.

   a. another place   b. the past   c. postwar times

9. What *else* do you want to do today?

   a. time   b. important   c. other thing

10. Will you *support* me with this new idea?

    a. prevent   b. help   c. show

C. Word Forms

DIRECTIONS: Look at the endings for <u>verbs</u> and <u>adjectives</u>. Are the italicized words in the sentences verbs or adjectives?

	VERBS	ADJECTIVES
	like	lik*able*
	accept	accept*able*

	VERB	ADJECTIVE
1. Ask anyone. Everyone here is very *knowledgeable.*	_____	_____
2. Her personality *changes* like the wind.	_____	_____
3. That solution is *unthinkable.*	_____	_____
4. What do Americans *value?*	_____	_____
5. He usually has very *changeable* ideas.	_____	_____
6. *Compare* the two cars. They are very similar.	_____	_____
7. This is a very strange place; the weather *changes* almost every hour.	_____	_____
8. Your decision is not *workable.*	_____	_____
9. Those two cars have *comparable* engines.	_____	_____
10. I know what you mean. It's *understandable.*	_____	_____

D. Speaking

DIRECTIONS: Answer the following questions and then share your answers with a classmate or with the class.

1. Did you grow up in a small community or in a large city?

2. How is life in your community different from what it was forty years ago?

3. What are the difficult problems for parents today? Number the following phrases in order of difficulty (1 is the most difficult).

_____ physical danger
_____ education
_____ drugs
_____ premarital sex
_____ loss of religion
_____ extreme religions
_____ alcohol

OTHER PROBLEMS

_____ _____
_____ _____
_____ _____
_____ _____

4. From the children's point of view, which of the problems above are the most difficult? You can probably think of some other problems young people have.

5. Can you think of any ways to make life easier for either parents or children? What are these ways?

E. Writing

DIRECTIONS: *A* contraction *is the shortening of two words. For example,* it's *is a contraction of* it is*. When we speak, we use many contractions. The reading in section 3 has many contractions. It is written as Ron speaks. Change the third paragraph by following the instructions below.*

(1) *Change* I *to* he*. Begin your paragraph with "Ron Perotta is a realist. He . . . ."*
(2) *Do not use contractions.*
(3) *Change the word* kids *to* children*. (*Kids *is a slang word.)*

Look Back

A. Vocabulary

DIRECTIONS: Circle the letter of the choice that best completes each sentence.

1. The _____ of new schools is important in developing countries.

   a. sociology   b. statistics   c. establishment

2. I know my friend is a little crazy sometimes, but _____ he is a good person.

   a. early   b. in relationships   c. basically

3. A lot of people live in my house and there is very little _____. I can't get away from the other people to be by myself.

   a. privacy   b. noise   c. socializing

4. There is too much crime and _____ on television shows today. I think it has a bad influence on children and on adults, too.

   a. divorce   b. privacy   c. violence

5. I don't know how to _____ this camera. My photographs are never clear.

   a. type   b. experience   c. focus

6. What is your _____ reason for coming here?

   a. primary   b. previous   c. realistic

7. In the _____ world, TV is an important means of communication.

   a. contemporary   b. statistical   c. violent

8. This writer always _____ descriptions of scenery. I like more action.

   a. prevents   b. emphasizes   c. reshapes

9. The situation is only _____; it will change soon.

   a. reality   b. partial   c. temporary

10. We always celebrate our holidays in the _____ way.

   a. traditional   b. supportive   c. experienced

B. Matching

DIRECTIONS: Find the word or phrase in column B which has a similar meaning to a word in column A. Write the letter of that word or phrase next to the word in column A.

	A		B
1. _____	prevent	a.	basic belief
2. _____	neighborhood	b.	repeated action requiring no thought
3. _____	habit	c.	closeness
4. _____	primary	d.	typical
5. _____	town	e.	stop before it happens
6. _____	togetherness	f.	area of places to live
7. _____	sense	g.	set up
8. _____	establish	h.	major
9. _____	value	i.	feeling
10. _____	common	j.	very small city

Answer Key
Section 1: **A.** 1. 2 2. 3 3. 4 4. 1 **C.** a. 1 b. 4 c. 3 d. 3 e. 3 f. 2 g. 1 h. 2 i. 2 j. 4 **D.** 1. different 2. different 3. similar 4. similar 5. similar 6. different 7. different 8. different 9. different 10. similar 11. different 12. different 13. similar 14. similar 15. different 16. different 17. similar 18. similar 19. similar 20. similar **E.** 1. b 2. b 3. b 4. a 5. b 6. a 7. c 8. a 9. b 10. b
Section 2: **A.** 1. b 2. c. 3. b 4. a 5. a 6. b 7. b 8. b 9. c 10. a **B.** 1. a 2. c 3. b 4. c 5. c 6. b 7. b 8. b 9. a 10. b
Section 3: **A.** 1. F 2. F 3. F 4. F 5. T 6. F 7. T 8. ITK 9. T 10. T **B.** 1. c 2. a 3. a 4. b 5. c 6. b 7. a 8. b 9. c 10. b **C.** 1. adjective 2. verb 3. adjective 4. verb 5. adjective 6. verb 7. verb 8. adjective 9. adjective 10. adjective
Section 4: **A.** 1. c 2. c 3. a 4. c 5. c 6. a 7. a 8. b 9. c 10. a **B.** 1. e 2. f 3. b 4. h 5. j 6. c 7. i 8. g 9. a 10. d

Retirement

A First Look

A. Main Idea

DIRECTIONS: *Before you begin to read, look at these main ideas. There is one main idea for each paragraph. Write the number of the paragraph next to the main idea of that paragraph. Work <u>very quickly</u>. Do not read every word at this point.*

1. ____3____ the financial problems of retirement

2. ____1____ the value of work in America

3. ____5____ answers to some problems

4. ____4____ the bright side of retirement

5. ____2____ explanation of retirement

B. Reading

DIRECTIONS: Now read carefully.

1

Work is a very important part of life in the United States. [1]
When the early Protestant immigrants came to this country, they [2]
brought the idea that work was the way to God and heaven. This [3]
attitude, the Protestant work ethic, still influences America today. [4]
Work is not only important for economic benefits, the salary, but [5]
also for social and psychological needs, the feeling of doing some- [6]
thing for the good of the society. Americans spend most of their lives [7]
working, being productive. For most Americans, their work defines [8]
them: They are what they do. What happens, then, when a person [9]
can no longer work? [10]

2

Most Americans stop working at age sixty-five or seventy and [11]
retire. Because work is such an important part of life in this culture, [12]
retirement can be very difficult. Retirees often feel that they are [13]
useless and unproductive. Of course, some people are happy to retire; [14]
but leaving one's job, whatever it is, is a difficult change, even for [15]

those who look forward to retiring. Many retirees do not know how   16
to use their time or they feel lost without their jobs.   17

Retirement can also bring financial problems. Many people   18
depend on Social Security checks every month. During their working   19
years, employees contribute a certain percentage of their salaries   20
to the government. Each employer also gives a certain percentage   21
to the government. When people retire, they receive this money as   22
income. These checks do not provide enough money to live on, how-   23
ever, because prices are increasing very rapidly. Senior citizens,   24
those over sixty-five, have to have savings in the bank or other   25
retirement plans to make ends meet. The rate of inflation is forcing   26
prices higher each year; Social Security checks alone cannot cover   27
these growing expenses. The government offers some assistance,   28
Medicare (health care) and welfare (general assistance), but many   29
senior citizens have to change their lifestyles after retirement. They   30
have to spend carefully to be sure that they can afford to buy food,   31
fuel, and other necessities.   32

Of course, many senior citizens are happy with retirement.   33
They have time to spend with their families or to enjoy their hobbies.   34
Some continue to work part time; others do volunteer work. Some,   35
like those in the Retired Business Executives Association, even help   36
young people to get started in new businesses. Many retired citizens   37
also belong to "Golden Age" groups. These organizations plan trips   38
and social events. There are many opportunities for retirees.   39

American society is only beginning to be concerned about the   40
special physical and emotional needs of its senior citizens. The gov-   41
ernment is taking steps to ease the problem of limited income. They   42
are building new housing, offering discounts in stores and museums   43
and on buses, and providing other services, such as free courses,   44
food service, and help with housework. Retired citizens are a rapidly   45
growing percentage of the population. This part of the population   46
is very important and we must respond to their needs. After all,   47
every citizen will be a senior citizen some day.   48

(In left margin: 3, 4, 5)

Reading Clue

7.1 Look at the sentence on lines 23 and 24. What
     does the word *because* introduce?
       (a) a reason
       (b) a result (conclusion)
       (c) a contrast (something different)
Look at page 224 for the answer.

C. Scanning

DIRECTIONS: Write the number of the paragraph where you find the following information.

a. _____ special physical and emotional needs

b. _____ at age sixty-five or seventy

c. _____ "Golden Age" groups

d. _____ work is important

e. _____ Medicare

f. _____ limited income

g. _____ volunteer work

h. _____ a difficult change

i. _____ to God and heaven

j. _____ free courses

D. Vocabulary

DIRECTIONS: Look at the following pairs of words. Find the word(s) on the left in the reading. Compare its meanings to the word(s) on the right. Are the words similar or different? Write similar or different on the line.

work (1)	job	1. _____ s _____
still (4)	no longer (10)	2. _____ d _____
ethic (4)	value	3. _____ s _____
economic (5)	financial (18)	4. _____ s _____
salary (5)	income (23)	5. _____ s _____
psychological (6)	physical (41)	6. _____ d _____
productive (8)	doing nothing	7. _____ d _____
useless (14)	productive (8)	8. _____ d _____
contribute (20)	take	9. _____ d _____
employer (21)	worker	10. _____ d _____
senior (24)	youngest	11. _____ d _____
make ends meet (26)	have enough	12. _____ s _____

afford (31)	be able to buy	13. ____s____
necessities (32)	needed things	14. ____s____
volunteer (35)	paid	15. ____d____
get started (37)	begin	16. ____s____
concerned (40)	worried	17. ____s____
providing (44)	offering	18. ____s____
discount (43)	higher price	19. ____d____
respond to (47)	answer	20. ____s____

E. Reading Comprehension

DIRECTIONS: Circle the letter of the choice that best completes each sentence.

1. The author believes that work became important to Americans because of ____ pressure.

   a. economic   b. religious   c. family

2. Protestants believed in ____ .

   a. high salaries   b. America   c. hard work

3. Senior citizens have to have other savings because Social Security checks ____ .

   a. are not enough   b. come monthly   c. cover growing expenses

4. When Americans stop work, it is difficult for them to ____ .

   a. feel productive   b. get Social Security checks   c. go to heaven

5. According to the author, ____ Americans stop work at age sixty-five or seventy.

   a. some   b. a few   c. most

6. The author mentions ____ examples of discounts.

   a. two   b. three   c. four

7. When people retire, they often ____ .

   a. have a lot of money   b. have to spend money carefully   c. feel useful and productive

8. The number of retired citizens is ____ .

   a. staying the same   b. increasing   c. decreasing

9. A salary is a(n) ____ benefit.

   a. psychological   b. social   c. economic

10. "Golden Age" groups plan ____ .

   a. opportunities   b. businesses   c. social activities

Look Again

A. Vocabulary

DIRECTIONS: Circle the letter of the choice that best completes each sentence.

1. Clothing is an example of a(n) ____ .

   a. assistance   b. necessity   c. concern

2. It is very late. She is very ____ about her son.

   a. productive   b. demanding   c. concerned

3. My ____ pays me a good salary.

   a. volunteer   b. employer   c. employee

4. Every year I ____ a percentage of my income to the Protestant church.

   a. limit   b. receive   c. contribute

5. Every year he ____ to work at the school fair; he never gets paid.

   a. gets by   b. volunteers   c. provides

6. The older children in a family always ____ the younger ones.

   a. establish   b. influence   c. define

7. I don't have enough money to buy a new car. I cannot ____ one.

   a. demand   b. provide   c. afford

8. Your salary is very low. Do you have any other ____?

   a. income   b. interest   c. percentage

9. His physical condition is unbelievable: he's seventy and he ____ jogs.

   a. no longer   b. then   c. still

10. He is a ____ volunteer here at the hospital; he is a big problem and no help.

    a. productive   b. useful   c. useless

B. Reading Comprehension

DIRECTIONS: Circle the letter of the choice that best completes each sentence.

1. ____ affects our feelings about work.

   a. Retirement   b. The Protestant ethic   c. Social Security

2. Many retirees feel useless because they ____ .

   a. do volunteer work   b. have limited incomes   c. aren't working

3. According to the author, many Americans define themselves by their ____ .

   a. salaries   b. needs   c. work

4. The author mentions "free courses" as an example of ____ .

   a. hobbies   b. government services   c. social events

5. The last sentence of the reading means that each person ____ .

   a. is important   b. is a citizen   c. will grow old

6. Retired people receive ____ each month.

   a. expenses   b. Social Security checks   c. salaries

7. Many people who retire feel unproductive because their work ____ .

   a. defined them   b. was unimportant   c. was difficult

8. The author believes that leaving a job is difficult for ____ people.

   a. some   b. many   c. a few

9. Medicare and welfare are examples of ____ .

   a. Social Security   b. other retirement plans   c. government help

10. Many senior citizens have to change their ____ .

    a. needs   b. lifestyles   c. opportunities

C. Questions

DIRECTIONS: Answer the following questions.

1. Why is work so important in the United States?

2. Why do you think that work was seen as the way to God?

3. How do people feel when they have to retire?

4. Explain some of the possible incomes for retirement.

5. What do some people who retire do with their free time?

6. What are some of the programs which the government is sponsoring for senior citizens?

Contact a Point of View

A. Timed Reading

DIRECTIONS: Read the following point of view and answer the questions in four minutes.

I retired about a year ago. The company had a big party for me; they gave me a gold watch for more than thirty years of service. At the party, everyone said to me, "Retirement is a time to do all the things you didn't have time to do. It's a new beginning." I can't say that I dislike retirement, but after working for thirty-five years, day after day, it's hard to adjust to all this free time.

Just after I retired, Peg and I went to visit John, Jr. in Chicago and Ann in New York. We really had a good time. We enjoy being together. In fact, John, Jr. invited us to come and live with him. He knows that living on Social Security checks and a small retirement plan is not easy. But we decided not to move in with him. We have our lives and he and his wife have theirs. We are going to stay here in town. We may move to an apartment, because the house is too big for only the two of us and it's hard to keep clean. Peg is having some trouble with her back; she's seeing the doctor tomorrow.

Money isn't a serious problem for us because we do have some savings, but we have to make careful decisions about what we can afford. We're not used to living on a fixed income, but we make ends meet. I still belong to the club and I play cards there once a week, and we spend time with other retired couples in the area. My only regret is that I didn't spend enough time thinking about retirement before it happened.

DIRECTIONS: *Read each of the following statements carefully to determine whether each is true, false, or impossible to know. Check the appropriate blank.*

	TRUE	FALSE	IMPOSSIBLE TO KNOW
1. This man retired about six months ago.		✓	
2. The people at the party were negative about retiring.		✓	
3. This man's son is married.	✓		
4. This man worked for forty years in the company.		✓	
5. He and his wife are moving in with John, Jr.		✓	
6. This man dislikes retirement.		✓	
7. He and his wife live only on their savings and a retirement plan.		✓	
8. This man has other children at home.		✓	
9. This man has some physical problems.			✓
10. They are going to move from the town.		✓	

B. Vocabulary

DIRECTIONS: Fill in the blanks with vocabulary from the reading. Make necessary changes in the form of the word.

1. serious/regret/plans

I have some _____ _____ about

my _____ to live away from my family.

2. in fact/begin/back/trouble

Little by little he is _____ to feel better.

_____ , he has no _____

at all with his _____ now.

3. dislike/decisions/money

I _____ making _____ about

_____ .

4. limited/afford/make ends meet

I can't _____ to live on a _____

income because I can't _____ .

C. Word Forms

DIRECTIONS: Choose the appropriate word form in each sentence.

1. special
   specialty

2. pain
   painful
   painless

3. simple
   simplicity

4. knowledge
   knowledgeable

5. beneficial
   benefit

6. cultural
   culture

1. What is the _____ of this restaurant?

2. What a _____ in the neck!

3. She is a _____ child.

4. Her _____ of physics surprised me.

5. It is _____ to visit another country.

6. Differences in _____ often cause serious trouble.

7. familiarity
   familiar

7. I was unaccustomed to the _____ in that society.

8. fear
   fearless
   fearful

8. He is without _____ .

9. impressionable
   impression

9. She is very young and _____ .

10. senseless
    sense

10. What is the real _____ of this word?

D. Speaking

DIRECTIONS: Show your opinion of the following statements by putting 1 next to your first preference, 2 next to your second choice, and so on through 6. Share your ideas with a classmate or the class.

When my parents grow old and retire, I hope that they live

_____ with me.

_____ with my brother.

_____ with my sister.

_____ some time with me, and some time with my brother and/or sister.

_____ near me, so I can visit them.

_____ independently of the family.

Often a real problem happens when one parent dies and the other is alone. If my father died, I'm sure that my mother would

_____ continue living where she is living.

_____ move in with me.

_____ live with my brother.

_____ live with my sister.

_____ move to a smaller residence.

_____ move to a nursing home (a home for the elderly).

E. Writing

Because introduces a reason or cause. A result follows.

> *reason*   *result*
> *Because he is sixty-five years old, he is retiring.*

A clause with because cannot stand alone. It must be completed.
Because he is sixty-five years old is not a sentence; there is no result.

Therefore is similar to *because* in meaning, but the form is different.

> *reason*   *result*
> *He is sixty-five years old; therefore, he is retiring.*

DIRECTIONS: Write each of the following sentences in two ways. Use <u>because</u> and then <u>therefore</u>.

Example: he volunteers/he doesn't get a salary

1. *Because he volunteers, he doesn't get a salary.*
2. *He volunteers; therefore, he doesn't get a salary.*

   1. she can't afford a new dress/she has to buy necessities

   2. my father is not a senior citizen yet/he is only fifty-five years old

   3. he is a productive worker/he believes in the Protestant work ethic

   4. my work is very important/I never take a vacation

   5. that family is having economic difficulties/each member has to contribute

Look Back

A. Vocabulary

DIRECTIONS: Circle the letter of the choice that best completes each sentence.

1. Poverty in a wealthy society is a(n) ____ problem.

   a. mobile   b. ethical   c. spacious

2. She is in her last year of high school. She is a ____ .

   a. junior   b. senior   c. beginner

3. A car is a(n) ____ in the suburbs.

   a. aspect   b. establishment   c. necessity

4. Don't worry. Everything will be fine. Heaven will ____ .

   a. produce   b. provide   c. make ends meet

5. This coat is ____ . You can have it with 15 percent off.

   a. salaried   b. increasing   c. discounted

6. The price of oil ____ daily.

   a. costs   b. inflates   c. develops

7. I can ____ with twenty dollars a day.

   a. afford   b. make ends meet   c. look for

8. This hat is ____ in the rain. It's too small and doesn't cover my head.

   a. fixed   b. useless   c. casual

9. Our culture ____ our thoughts and actions.

   a. influences   b. gets started   c. contains

10. He's a very good student. ____ , he's the best in the class.

    a. For example   b. In fact   c. Therefore

B. Matching

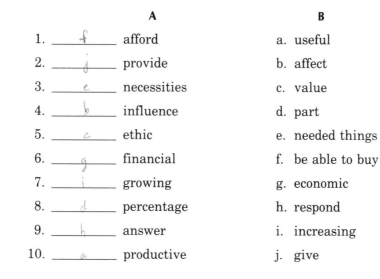

	A		B
1.	__f__ afford	a.	useful
2.	__j__ provide	b.	affect
3.	__e__ necessities	c.	value
4.	__b__ influence	d.	part
5.	__c__ ethic	e.	needed things
6.	__g__ financial	f.	be able to buy
7.	__i__ growing	g.	economic
8.	__d__ percentage	h.	respond
9.	__h__ answer	i.	increasing
10.	__a__ productive	j.	give

chapter 8

Equality for All?

section 1 ————————————————————————

A First Look

A. Main Idea

DIRECTIONS: *Before you begin to read, look at these main ideas. There is one main idea for each paragraph. Write the number of the paragraph next to the main idea of that paragraph. Work <u>very quickly</u>. Do not read every word at this point.*

1. _____2_____ American society
2. _____6_____ more about discrimination
3. _____4_____ equal opportunity laws
4. _____1_____ questions about possibilities for minorities
5. _____5_____ definitions of prejudice and discrimination
6. _____3_____ examples of self-made men

B. Reading

DIRECTIONS: *Now read carefully.*

1   Can a poor country boy from the hills of Kentucky become President of the United States? Can a poor, black, city boy become wealthy and famous all over the world? Can a woman become President of the United States? The answer to all of these questions is "yes, ideally it is possible." The key word here is "ideally." Ideally, everyone in the United States, whether rich or poor, has an equal opportunity to succeed.

2   This concept of equal opportunity to succeed is a basic idea in capitalism, the economic system of the United States. Social classes or levels are not permanently established. The terms *upper class* or *upper-middle class* are mainly financial terms, although an upper-class person has been wealthy for a long time. There are no kings, queens, or other royalty in the United States, and a person's back-

1
2
3
4
5
6
7
8
9
10
11
12
13

ground is not as important as that person's position now. Perhaps 14
because the United States is a country of immigrants, people who 15
often had very little when they arrived in the country, Americans 16
value the ability to go "from rags to riches." 17

3 The first two examples in the first paragraph are descriptions 18
of self-made men, who started life with almost nothing and became 19
successful. These men are President Abraham Lincoln and the boxer 20
Mohammed Ali. These two men did not have the advantages of 21
wealth, good educational opportunities, or contact with powerful 22
people. However, they were ambitious and wanted to succeed. 23

Of course, it is unrealistic to say that everyone who wants to 24
succeed will be able to succeed. But there are laws which give every 25
person in the United States the chance or opportunity to succeed. 26
These laws guarantee equal opportunities for education and em- 27
ployment to all people. These laws are especially important to mem- 28
4 bers of minorities (i.e., any group of people not white, Protestant, 29
and male in the United States) such as Hispanics, women, blacks, 30
and many other ethnic, religious, and racial groups. Minority groups 31
may find that they do not have equal education, housing, or em- 32
ployment. They may have difficulty finding jobs or getting adequate 33
pay because of prejudice. 34

Prejudice is a negative feeling against a person because of his 35
or her race, religion, or background. For example, if a factory owner 36
does not like Mexican-Americans in general, this person is preju- 37
diced. A prejudiced person actually prejudges a whole group of people 38
and feels negatively about all the people in that group. If a factory 39
5 owner feels prejudiced, this is not a problem. The problem arises 40
when this factory owner refuses to hire someone because of preju- 41
dice. If an employer gives a job to a man instead of a women when 42
both are equally qualified, this is called discrimination. Discrimi- 43
nation in housing, education, and employment is illegal in this 44
country. 45

The word *discrimination* really means the observation of dif- 46
ferences. Obviously, there are differences in people. However, equal 47
6 opportunity laws try to prevent differences from becoming problems 48
when people want to succeed. In education, employment, and many 49
other areas, discrimination is a bad word. 50

Reading Clue

8.1 Find an expression in line 24 and a word in line
47 that introduce information the writer thinks
is common knowledge.
What are these words?
Look at page 224 for the answer.

C. Scanning

DIRECTIONS: Write the number of the paragraph where you find the following information.

a. _____ Hispanics

b. _____ a factory owner

c. _____ self-made men

d. _____ especially important to members of minorities

e. _____ "from rags to riches"

f. _____ prevent differences from becoming problems

g. _____ the key word

h. _____ Mohammed Ali

i. _____ when both are equally qualified

j. _____ whether rich or poor

D. Vocabulary

DIRECTIONS: Look at the following pairs of words. Find the word on the left in the reading.
Compare its meaning to the word(s) on the right. Are the words similar or different?
Write similar or different on the line.

country (1)	city	1. ___d___
key (5)	important	2. ___s___
ideally (5)	really	3. ___d___

equal (6)	same	4. _____s_____
opportunity (7)	chance (26)	5. _____s_____
capitalism (9)	economic system (9)	6. _____s_____
class (10,11)	level (10)	7. _____s_____
wealthy (12)	poor (6)	8. _____d_____
rags (17)	riches (17)	9. _____d_____
start (19)	finish	10. _____d_____
advantage (21)	benefit	11. _____s_____
unrealistic (24)	realistic	12. _____d_____
succeed (25)	do well	13. _____s_____
guarantee (27)	promise	14. _____s_____
adequate (33)	enough	15. _____s_____
pay (34)	salary	16. _____s_____
prejudice (35)	feeling (35)	17. _____s_____
refuse (41)	agree	18. _____d_____
qualified (43)	able	19. _____s_____
illegal (44)	legal	20. _____d_____

E. Reading Comprehension

DIRECTIONS: Circle the letter of the choice that best completes each sentence.

1. According to the author, a woman _____ become President of the United States.

   a. can never   b. can ideally   c. probably will not

2. Abraham Lincoln and Mohammed Ali _____ examples of self-made men.

   a. are   b. knew   c. contacted

3. Abraham Lincoln and Mohammed Ali were born _____.

   a. rich   b. black   c. poor

4. Lincoln and Ali succeeded _____ wealth, good educational opportunities, and powerful friends.

   a. because of   b. in order to get   c. without

5. According to the author, everyone who wants to succeed ____ succeed.

   a. will be able to   b. cannot   c. has to

6. Generally speaking, social classes in the United States are ____.

   a. permanently   b. royalty   c. financial divisions
      established

7. Women ____ considered a minority in the United States in terms of discrimination.

   a. are not   b. usually are not   c. are

8. If you think someone did not give you a job because of prejudice, you should ____.

   a. forget it   b. contact a lawyer   c. feel like a minority member

9. It is ____ to refuse to give someone a job because of race, religion, or sex.

   a. intelligent   b. illegal   c. guaranteed

10. According to the author, all people in the United States ____.

   a. have some chance   b. are equal   c. are minorities
      of success

Look Again

A. Vocabulary

DIRECTIONS: Circle the letter of the choice that best completes each sentence.

1. What is the ____ for your negative feeling? Why do you feel that way?

   a. president   b. observation   c. basis

2. A famous person is a person ____ knows.

   a. everybody   b. somebody   c. nobody

3. A king and queen are members of ____.

   a. immigrants   b. royalty   c. employment

4. ____ is not a member of a minority in the United States.

   a. A black Puerto Rican   b. A white male   c. A female

5. The food was adequate. Everyone had ____ to eat.

   a. a lot   b. very little   c. the right amount

6. A person who is prejudiced against Hispanics has a (n) ____ feeling about them.

   a. negative   b. beneficial   c. advantageous

7. I want a job. Will you ____ me in your company?

   a. provide   b. succeed   c. hire

8. She refused. Her answer was ____.

   a. positive   b. negative   c. prejudice

9. I bought the house because I plan to live here ____.

   a. permanently   b. negatively   c. unrealistically

10. Discrimination in housing means that a landlord does not rent because ____.

    a. there is no apartment available   b. the people are unpleasant   c. of prejudice

B. Reading Comprehension

DIRECTIONS: Circle the letter of the choice that best completes each sentence.

1. According to the author, a woman ____ become President of the United States.

   a. will never   b. may   c. will definitely

2. It is ____ to succeed without wealth, education, and contact with powerful people.

   a. easy   b. impossible   c. difficult

3. Americans value the concept of equal opportunity because ____ .

   a. many Americans   b. Americans like money   c. many poor immigrants
      are wealthy   became rich

4. There ____ laws which guarantee equal opportunity.

   a. are no   b. should be   c. are

5. According to the reading, a person who has the opportunity to succeed ____ succeed.

   a. will usually   b. will not always   c. will never

6. ____ is illegal.

   a. Discrimination   b. A minority   c. Prejudice

7. Discrimination is a problem because it does not give people ____ .

   a. the same chance   b. an easy life   c. prejudice
      to succeed

8. Women ____ the same pay as men in similar jobs.

   a. do not always get   b. always get   c. never get

9. Equal opportunity is important in ____ .

   a. capitalism   b. social class   c. position

10. The author thinks that ____ .

    a. there is equality in b. prejudice is illegal   c. discrimination is a
       the United States   serious problem

C. Questions

DIRECTIONS: Answer the following questions.

1. Give two examples of discrimination.

2. What is capitalism?

3. Give three examples of minorities.

4. What is the difference between upper-middle class and upper class?

5. What are equal opportunity laws?

Contact a Point of View

A. Timed Reading

DIRECTIONS: Read the following point of view and answer the questions in four minutes.

Silvia Garcia, a black woman, applied for a job at a small company. One question on the application form was "Who else lives at your home address?" Ms. Garcia did not answer this question. She left the space blank.

The owner of the company, Jeff Erler, was a very religious man. He had started the company himself and felt that his employees were like his extended family. Mr. Erler interviewed Ms. Garcia personally. He noticed that she had marked "single" on her application and he was surprised that she was not married at her age. When he mentioned this to her, she just laughed and did not comment. He decided that she was a very nice woman. He also needed to hire members of minorities, so he hired her.

Ms. Garcia did very well in the company. In a few months she got a raise and was happy with the additional money. However, seven months after Mr. Erler hired her, he overheard a conversation in the cafeteria. Two other workers were talking about her and "the guy she's living with."

Mr. Erler called Ms. Garcia into his office that afternoon. He questioned her about her living situation and she admitted that she was living with her boyfriend. Mr. Erler told her that he was very sorry, but he did not want immoral people to work in his company. At first, she could not believe that Mr. Erler was serious. She told him that he had no right to call her immoral because she was living with her boyfriend. She said that as long as she was a good worker, her personal life was her own business and that he could not make judgments about it. Mr. Erler fired Ms. Garcia.

DIRECTIONS: *Read each of the following sentences carefully to determine whether each is true, false, or impossible to know. Check the appropriate blank.*

	TRUE	FALSE	IMPOSSIBLE TO KNOW
1. Ms. Garcia was a member of a minority group.	✓		
2. When Ms. Garcia applied for the job, she lived with her boyfriend.	✓		
3. Ms. Garcia was not a good worker.		✓	
4. Mr. Erler was a religious man.	✓		
5. All Mr. Erler's employees were religious.			✓
6. Ms. Garcia's boyfriend worked in the same company.			✓
7. No one at the company except Mr. Erler knew that Ms. Garcia was living with someone.		✓	

	TRUE	FALSE	IMPOSSIBLE TO KNOW
8. Ms. Garcia told Mr. Erler that she was not living with her boyfriend.		✓	
9. Ms. Garcia was thirty years old.			✓
10. Ms. Garcia lost her job at Mr. Erler's company.	✓		

B. Vocabulary

DIRECTIONS: Circle the letter of the word(s) with the same meaning as the italicized word(s).

1. Who *else* lives at this address?

    a. related   b. in addition   c. only

2. The page was *blank*.

    a. empty   b. written   c. full

3. Leave a *space* between the lines of our compositions.

    a. meaning   b. certain area   c. sentence

4. I *applied* for a loan at the bank.

    a. questioned   b. gave money   c. tried to get

5. A politician often says, "*No comment*."

    a. I have nothing to say   b. I don't know   c. Don't talk to me

6. Our office *hired* someone just yesterday.

    a. fired   b. gave more money to   c. gave a job to

7. I spoke with the director *personally*.

    a. myself   b quickly   c. immediately

8. Her *personal* life is very interesting.

    a. social   b. private   c. love

9. If he steals money from poor people, he is *immoral*.

    a. rich   b. arrested   c. without values

10. I need a *raise*. I cannot support myself with this salary.

    a. job   b. higher pay for the same job   c. vacation with more money

C. Word Forms

DIRECTIONS: *Look at the endings below for nouns and verbs. Are the italicized words in the sentences <u>nouns</u> or <u>verbs</u>?*

NOUNS	VERBS
produc*tion*	produce
adjust*ment*	adjust
real*ity*	rea*lize*

	NOUN	VERB
1. I'll help you *familiarize* yourself with the city.	_____	_____
2. *Discrimination* in hiring is illegal.	_____	_____
3. How did you *solve* that problem?	_____	_____
4. Could you *repeat* that please?	_____	_____
5. I made an *adjustment* in the plan.	_____	_____
6. I don't have a *solution* to that problem.	_____	_____
7. His *identity* is still a question.	_____	_____
8. What is your *community* like?	_____	_____
9. We can't *produce* that many machines.	_____	_____
10. Can you *identify* the problem?	_____	_____

D. Speaking

DIRECTIONS: *Reread the information about Silvia Garcia and Jeff Erler. Then answer the following questions and share your ideas with the class.*

1. What do you think Ms. Garcia does next?

    _____ collects unemployment insurance?
    _____ looks for another job?
    _____ goes to see a lawyer?
    _____ _____?

2. Do you think that Mr. Erler was fair to Ms. Garcia?

3. Do you think that Mr. Erler did anything illegal when he fired her?

4. Did Mr. Erler discriminate against her because of:
   her race?
   her sex?
   her religion?
   her personal background?
   her moral values?

5. Do you think this is discrimination? Is it an unfair employment procedure?

Optional Activity

If you decide that this case is an example of discrimination or unfair employment procedures, take it to court. Act out the parts of these people:
   Silvia Garcia
   Steve Kennedy, Silvia's boyfriend
   Jeff Erler
   Alice Lee, Jeff's secretary
   The lawyers who help Silvia Garcia
   The lawyers who help Jeff Erler
   A judge, who also organizes the trial
   A jury of people who decide the final judgment

Step 1: Meet in groups to decide what roles and positions you will take.
Step 2: Meet in court and present the evidence.
Step 3: Wait for the jury's decision.

E. Writing

DIRECTIONS: What happened to Silvia Garcia and Jeff Erler? Write a fifth paragraph to finish the story.

Look Back

A. Vocabulary

DIRECTIONS: Circle the letter of the choice that best completes each sentence.

1. The ____ man did not like his daughter's boyfriend because he was Chinese.

   a. prejudiced   b. advantageous   c. adequate

2. I don't know if this color is green or gray. I don't have very good color ____ .

   a. prejudice   b. discrimination   c. equality

3. There were two men and twelve women in the class. The men were in the ____ .

   a. minority   b. percentage   c. opportunity

4. I found a job easily because my father ____ me to work for him.

   a. hired   b. gave   c. refused

5. I decided to quit before the owner ____ me.

   a. raised   b. fired   c. felt

6. With a degree in business, she was highly ____ to work in the company.

   a. qualified   b. adequate   c. prejudiced

7. There is a six-month ____ on this radio. If it breaks in that time, you can get another one for free.

   a. age   b. guarantee   c. qualification

8. I ____ a raise. I don't know if I will get one or not.

   a. prevented   b. fired   c. applied for

9. I can't ____ him. He doesn't answer his phone.

   a. adjust to   b. contact   c. give

10. I am very ____ . I want to succeed and be at the top of my profession.

    a. ambitious   b. economic   c. self-made

B. Matching

DIRECTIONS: Find the word or phrase in column B which has a similar meaning to a word in column A. Write the letter of that word or phrase next to the word in column A.

A		B
1. _f_ succeed		a. smaller group
2. _b_ illegal		b. not legal
3. _e_ opportunity		c. give a job to
4. _a_ minority		d. enough
5. _g_ refuse		e. chance
6. _d_ adequate		f. do well
7. _c_ hire		g. say no
8. _j_ employee		h. even though
9. _h_ although		i. the same
10. _i_ equal		j. worker in a company or business

chapter 9

Racial Issues

A First Look

A. Main Idea

DIRECTIONS: *Before you begin to read, look at these main ideas. There is one main idea for each paragraph. Write the number of the paragraph next to the main idea of that paragraph. Work <u>very quickly</u>. Do not read every word at this point.*

1. ___3___ prejudice in the South

2. ___1___ prejudice and discrimination are part of the United States

3. ___5___ equal education

4. ___7___ time is the answer

5. ___4___ discrimination in the North

6. ___6___ equal employment

7. ___2___ blacks compared to other groups

B. Reading

DIRECTIONS: *Now read carefully.*

1   Ironically, in the United States, a country of immigrants, prejudice and discrimination continue to be serious problems. There was often tension between each established group of immigrants and each succeeding group. As each group became more financially successful, and more powerful, they excluded newcomers from full participation in the society. Prejudice and discrimination are part of our history; however, this prejudicial treatment of different groups is nowhere more unjust than with black Americans.

    Blacks had distinct disadvantages. For the most part, they came to the "land of opportunity" as slaves and they were not free to keep their heritage and cultural traditions. Unlike most European immigrants, blacks did not have the protection of a support

1
2
3
4
5
6
7
8
9
10
11
12

2 group; sometimes slave owners separated members of the same family. They could not mix easily with the established society either because of their skin color. It was difficult for them to adapt to the American culture. Even after they became free people, they still experienced discrimination in employment, housing, education, and even in public facilities, such as restrooms.

3 Until the twentieth century (1900s), the majority of the black population lived in the southern part of the United States. Then there was a population shift to the large cities in the North. Prejudice against blacks is often associated with the South. Slavery was more common there and discrimination was usually more blatant (easier to see): Water fountains, restrooms, and restaurants were often designated "white only."

4 In the North, discrimination was usually less obvious, but certainly it created poor black neighborhoods, ghettos, in most large cities. This happened because of discrimination in housing and the movement of white city residents to the suburbs, often called "white flight."

5 In the 1950s and 1960s, blacks fought to gain fair treatment, and they now have legal protection in housing, education, and employment. Because their neighborhoods are segregated, many blacks feel that educational opportunities are not adequate for their children. Busing children from one neighborhood to another is one solution to inequality in education. Naturally, all parents want the best possible education for their children.

6 One attempt to equalize employment and educational opportunities for blacks and other minorities is "affirmative action." Affirmative action means that those in charge of businesses, organizations, and institutions should take affirmative (positive) action to find minorities to fill jobs. Many whites are angry about this regulation, because very qualified people sometimes do not get jobs when they are filled by people from a certain minority. People sometimes call this practice "reverse discrimination."

7 The situation of blacks is better today than it was in the 1950s, but racial tension persists. Time will be the real solution to the problem of race.

9.1 Look at line 10. What do the quotation marks
("|") around "land of opportunity" mean? The
writer believes that this expression is
(a) false.
(b) true.
(c) important.
Look at page 224 for the answer.

C. Scanning

DIRECTIONS: Write the number of the paragraph where you find the following information.

a. _____ prejudice associated with the South

b. _____ distinct disadvantages

c. _____ unlike most European immigrants

d. _____ time is the real solution

e. _____ equalize employment

f. _____ "reverse discrimination"

g. _____ before the 1900s

h. _____ more blatant discrimination

i. _____ the best possible education

j. _____ prejudice is part of our history

D. Vocabulary

DIRECTIONS: Look at the following pairs of words. Find the word on the left in the reading. Compare its meaning to the word(s) on the right. Are the words similar or different? Write similar *or* different *on the line.*

ironically (1)	naturally	1. _____d_____
continue (2)	persist	2. _____s_____

serious (2)	easy	3. _____ d _____
tension (3)	conflict	4. _____ s _____
succeeding (4)	going before	5. _____ d _____
financially (4)	economically	6. _____ s _____
excluded (5)	kept out	7. _____ s _____
participation (5–6)	involvement	8. _____ s _____
treatment (7)	action toward	9. _____ s _____
unjust (8)	fair	10. _____ d _____
disadvantage (9)	advantage	11. _____ d _____
slaves (10)	free people (16)	12. _____ d _____
heritage (11)	cultural past	13. _____ s _____
protection (12)	safety	14. _____ s _____
separate (13)	divide	15. _____ s _____
majority (19)	minority	16. _____ d _____
associated (22)	connected with	17. _____ s _____
blatant (23)	hidden	18. _____ d _____
designated (25)	chosen	19. _____ s _____
legal (32)	illegal	20. _____ d _____
segregated (33)	mixed	21. _____ d _____
inequality (36)	fairness	22. _____ d _____
attempt (38)	effort	23. _____ s _____
qualified (43)	capable	24. _____ s _____
reverse (45)	opposite	25. _____ s _____

E. Reading Comprehension

DIRECTIONS: Circle the letter of the choice that best completes each sentence.

1. Because of ____, blacks could not easily mix in American society.

   a. skin color   b. language   c. heritage

2. Special restrooms and water fountains for blacks were more common in ____.

   a. the North   b. ghettos   c. the South

3. An attempt to equalize education is ____ .

   a. reverse discrimination   b. white flight   c. busing

4. The Civil War took place in the 1860s, in the ____ century.

   a. twentieth   b. nineteenth   c. eighteenth

5. Slavery lasted longer and was more important in ____ .

   a. the 1950s and 1960s   b. the South   c. employment

6. Blacks were different from other groups because they ____ .

   a. came with the first   b. adapted easily   c. did not have support
      settlers   groups

7. There ____ discrimination in the North.

   a. was   b. wasn't   c. had to be

8. According to the author, there will be a solution to racial problems ____ .

   a. in the future   b. very soon   c. because of the 1950s

9. Affirmative action is a(n) ____ regulation.

   a. housing   b. employment   c. public facility

10. There was a population shift to the ____ in the early 1900s.

   a. suburbs   b. cities in the North   c. South

Look Again

A. Vocabulary

DIRECTIONS: Circle the letter of the choice that best completes each sentence.

1. I love to eat; ____, I hate to cook.

   a. ironically   b. naturally   c. financially

2. One ____ of city living is the high cost.

   a. advantage   b. benefit   c. disadvantage

3. He was ____ from the club because of his religious beliefs.

   a. participated   b. excluded   c. designated

4. Whites in the United States are the ____.

   a. minority   b. majority   c. newcomers

5. The cruel ____ of slaves in the United States is difficult to believe.

   a. treatment   b. protection   c. heritage

6. Although she didn't like him, he ____ in calling her.

   a. associated   b. persisted   c. designated

7. Busing is a(n) ____ to equalize educational opportunities.

   a. loss   b. attempt   c. participation

8. ____ schools are not legal.

   a. Integrated   b. Associated   c. Segregated

9. He is ____ to teach economics.

   a. adequate   b. qualified   c. obvious

10. ____ discrimination is clear and easy to see.

    a. Reverse   b. Blatant   c. Unjust

B. Reading Comprehension

DIRECTIONS: Circle the letter of the choice that best completes each sentence.

1. The author thinks that prejudice and discrimination ____ in the United States.

   a. are natural
   b. are the same for all groups
   c. form part of history

2. When Italian immigrants came to the United States, they probably ____ .

   a. were financially successful
   b. experienced discrimination
   c. participated fully in the society

3. Affirmative action is *most* beneficial for ____ .

   a. minorities
   b. business
   c. qualified people

4. ____ were created, in part, by "white flight."

   a. Neighborhoods
   b. Ghettos
   c. Large cities

5. Physically, blacks could not mix easily into the established society because ____ .

   a. they were newcomers
   b. of skin color
   c. of loss of heritage

6. Restrooms are examples of ____ .

   a. housing for the elderly
   b. public facilities
   c. slavery

7. In the North, discrimination was ____ to see.

   a. easier
   b. more difficult
   c. less difficult

8. The author thinks that prejudice is ironic here because the United States is a country of ____ .

   a. wealth
   b. immigrants
   c. established groups

9. Before 1900, the black population in the North was relatively ____ .

   a. large
   b. mixed
   c. small

10. The author speaks about ____ different areas of discrimination in paragraph 2.

   a. two
   b. three
   c. four

C. Questions

DIRECTIONS: Answer the following questions.

1. How were black immigrants different from other immigrants to the United States?

2. Why is prejudice so ironic in the United States?

3. Why do you think there are differences between the North and the South concerning racial prejudice?

4. Where do you think a large percentage of blacks live now?

5. Is there racial prejudice in your country? What are people doing about it?

Contact a Point of View

A. Timed Reading

DIRECTIONS: Read the following point of view and answer the questions in four minutes.

A few years ago, a man named Smith wanted to attend medical school in Washington. He applied and was not accepted, even though he had a university grade point average of 3.5. (At most universities, grades are from 4.0 to 0.0. 4.0 equals A, or excellent.) He was very upset that he was not accepted. He later discovered that some applicants had lower grade averages than he had: 2.5 and even 2.1. He also learned that these students were accepted because of their race. The medical school had an affirmative action policy that required filling a certain percentage of the places in each class with minority students. The school accepted these students with lower grade point averages to equalize the educational opportunities for minority students. They hoped that by accepting a certain number of minority students they could change a long history of discrimination.

Mr. Smith felt that this affirmative action policy was unjust, that he had the right to attend this medical school. He felt that he was better qualified and that the action of the medical school was reverse discrimination. He considered the action illegal and decided to bring his problem to the court for a decision.

He brought the issue to two state courts in Washington. The decision of the judges was that the action of the medical school was perfectly legal and that Smith had to accept this decision.

He then decided to bring the problem to the United States Supreme Court, where the final decision-making power in the United States lies. What do you think happened?

DIRECTIONS: *Read each of the following statements carefully to determine whether each is true, false, or impossible to know. Check the appropriate blank.*

	TRUE	FALSE	IMPOSSIBLE TO KNOW
1. Smith's average was better than most others.	✓		
2. His grade point average was high.	✓		
3. The two state courts said that the action was illegal.		✓	
4. This case happened last year.		✓	
5. Reverse discrimination means not accepting minorities.		✓	
6. The Supreme Court makes final decisions about laws in the United States.	✓		
7. Smith had no alternative after the decision of the two lower (state) courts.		✓	
8. The policy of the school was to fill all places with minority students.		✓	

	TRUE	FALSE	IMPOSSIBLE TO KNOW
9. Some students were accepted with less than 3.0 as a grade point average.	✓	_____	_____
10. There were minority students with higher averages than Smith's.	_____	_____	✓

B. Vocabulary

DIRECTIONS: Fill in the blanks with vocabulary from the reading.

1. attended/applied/accepted

   He _____ to Harvard but he was not _____ because there were so many applicants. He _____ the state university.

2. considered/judge/illegal/discrimination

   The _____ _____ that _____ in any form was _____.

3. qualified/applicants/grades

   _____ with _____ of 3.5 or more were _____.

4. policy/attempt

   This _____ was an _____ to equalize opportunities.

C. Word Forms

DIRECTIONS: Choose the appropriate word form for each sentence. Is it a noun or a verb?

1. employ
   employment
   1. She is looking for _____.

2. Discriminate
   Discrimination
   2. _____ is unfortunately part of the history of this country.

3. treat
   treatment
   3. What is the best way to _____ a cold?

4. educate
   education

4. Public schools should _____ everybody.

5. protect
   protection

5. Don't worry. I'll _____ you.

6. equalize
   equality

6. Is the basis of democracy _____?

7. associate
   association

7. She denies any _____ with him.

8. designate
   designation

8. The _____ of "white only" facilities is now over.

9. act
   action

9. They always _____ natural.

10. solve
    solution

10. Time isn't going to _____ this problem.

D. Speaking

DIRECTIONS: Mr. Smith's affirmative action case is a difficult one. According to the facts, what would you decide?
Get into groups of five and decide the case as the Supreme Court did. Remember that you must have a majority decision (3 to 2). After reaching your decision, present it to the class. Here is some useful vocabulary.

We feel that . . .

We agree that . . .

Mr. Smith should . . .   legal/illegal

The university should . . .   necessary/unnecessary

All applicants should . . .   unconstitutional

Minority applicants must . . .

Racial discrimination . . .

Reverse discrimination . . .

E. Writing

DIRECTIONS: *Now write about your decision. Explain why you made this decision.**

* See the answer key, page 141, for the actual Supreme Court decision.

Look Back

A. Vocabulary

DIRECTIONS: Circle the letter of the choice that best completes each sentence.

1. The woman did not want the magazines, but the salesman was ____ .

   a. exclusive   b. protective   c. persistent

2. This paper from the state court is filled with ____ .

   a. tension   b. legalities   c. loss

3. She has everything in order: She ____ her work very carefully.

   a. segregates   b. organizes   c. associates

4. She makes all the important company decisions, all the ____ ones.

   a. reverse   b. major   c. minor

5. It is ____ to do that now. Don't wait.

   a. blatant   b. advantageous   c. succeeding

6. ____ speaking, I don't understand the situation at all.

   a. Unjustly   b. Continuously   c. Seriously

7. He ____ Boston with Irish Catholics.

   a. associates   b. participates   c. discriminates

8. Cats are very ____ of their kittens.

   a. protective   b. serious   c. affirmative

9. He has improved 100 percent. He has made great ____ .

   a. attempts   b. gains   c. losses

10. He has very ____ taste; only the best for him.

    a. regulatory   b. discriminating   c. common

B. Matching

	A		B
1. _g_	naturally	a.	unfair
2. _h_	disadvantage	b.	positive
3. _e_	adequate	c.	tied with
4. _i_	legal	d.	different
5. _n_	participation	e.	enough
6. _o_	segregate	f.	easy to see
7. _a_	unjust	g.	obviously
8. _k_	qualified	h.	problem
9. _c_	associated	i.	lawful
10. _f_	blatant	j.	continue
11. _l_	serious	k.	able
12. _m_	majority	l.	important
13. _d_	distinct	m.	larger percentage
14. _j_	persist	n.	involvement
15. _b_	affirmative	o.	separate

Answer Key

Section 1: **A.** 1. 3 2. 1 3. 5 4. 7 5. 4 6. 6 7. 2 **C.** a. 3 b. 2 c. 2 d. 7 e. 6 f. 6 g. 3 h. 3 i. 5 j. 1 **D.** 1. different 2. similar 3. different 4. similar 5. different 6. similar 7. similar 8. similar 9. similar 10. different 11. different 12. different 13. similar 14. similar 15. similar 16. different 17. similar 18. different 19. similar 20. different 21. different 22. different 23. similar 24. similar 25. similar **E.** 1. a 2. c 3. c 4. b 5. b 6. c 7. a 8. a 9. b 10. b

Section 2: **A.** 1. a 2. c 3. b 4. b 5. a 6. b 7. b 8. c 9. b 10. b **B.** 1. c 2. b 3. a 4. b 5. b 6. b 7. b 8. b 9. c 10. c

Section 3: **A.** 1. T 2. T 3. F 4. F 5. F 6. T 7. F 8. F 9. T 10. ITK **B.** 1. applied, accepted, attended 2. judge, considered, discrimination, illegal 3. Applicants, grades, qualified 4. policy, attempt (*On June 28, 1978, the Supreme Court decided that reverse discrimination was illegal.) **C.** 1. employment 2. Discrimination 3. treat 4. educate 5. protect 6. equality 7. association 8. designation 9. act 10. solve

Section 4: **A.** 1. c 2. b 3. b 4. b 5. b 6. c 7. a 8. a 9. b 10. b **B.** 1. g 2. h 3. e 4. i 5. n 6. o 7. a 8. k 9. c 10. f 11. l 12. m 13. d 14. j 15. b

chapter 10

The Role of Women in the United States

A First Look

A. Main Idea

DIRECTIONS: *Before you begin to read, look at these main ideas. There is one main idea for each paragraph. Write the number of the paragraph next to the main idea of that paragraph. Work very quickly. Do not read every word at this point.*

1. _____5_____ life in the suburbs

2. _____1_____ a general description of American women

3. _____6_____ the current role of American women

4. _____2_____ life for a colonial woman

5. _____4_____ women in industry and business

6. _____3_____ women immigrants and ones who moved west

B. Reading

DIRECTIONS: *Now read carefully.*

1   American women experience a great variety of lifestyles. A "typical" American woman may be single. She may also be divorced or married. She may be a housewife, a doctor, or a factory worker. It is very difficult to generalize about American women. However, the one thing which differentiates American women from the women in other countries is their attitude about themselves and their role in American life.

      Historically, American women have always been very independent. The first colonists to come to New England were often young couples who had left behind their extended family (i.e., their parents, sisters, cousins, etc.). The women were alone in a new, undeveloped country with their husbands. This had two important effects. First of all, this as yet uncivilized environment demanded

2   that every person share in developing it and in survival. Women   *14*
worked alongside their husbands and children to establish them-   *15*
selves in this new land. Second, because they were in a new land   *16*
without the established influence of older members of society,   *17*
women felt free to step into nontraditional roles. In addition, there   *18*
were no rules in the Protestant religion which demanded that   *19*
women stay in any definite role.   *20*

This strong role of women was reinforced in later years as   *21*
Americans moved west, again leaving family behind and encoun-   *22*
tering a hostile environment. Even later, in the East, as new im-   *23*
3   migrants arrived, the women often found jobs more easily than men.   *24*
Women became the supporters of the family. The children of these   *25*
early Americans grew up with many examples of strong women   *26*
around them.   *27*

Within the established lifestyle of industrialized nineteenth-   *28*
and twentieth-century America, the strong role of women was not   *29*
as dramatic as in the early days of the country. Some women were   *30*
active outside the home; others were not. However, when American   *31*
4   men went to war in the 1940s, women stepped into the men's jobs   *32*
as factory and business workers. After the war, some women stayed   *33*
in these positions, and others left their jobs with a new sense of   *34*
their own capabilities.   *35*

When men returned from the war and the postwar "baby boom"   *36*
began, Americans began to move in great numbers to the suburbs.   *37*
A new model of a traditional family developed, and women were   *38*
essentially separated from men. Men generally went back into the   *39*
city to work, and there was a strong division between work and   *40*
home. Houses in the suburbs were far apart from each other, and   *41*
these areas were all residential; there were no stores or businesses.   *42*
5   Women had to drive to buy food and to visit family and friends. All   *43*
these factors contributed to a sense of isolation and to a feeling of   *44*
separation between the family and the outside world. At the same   *45*
time technological developments gave American housewives many   *46*
time-saving inventions such as dishwashers, vacuum cleaners, and   *47*
frozen foods. Life became easier for American housewives but not   *48*
necessarily more satisfying. With more time on their hands, Amer-   *49*
ican women began to want to become more involved.   *50*

Many people think that the women's movement, a political and   *51*
social effort to give women the same status and rights as men, is   *52*
a result of this isolation and separation of women in the suburbs.   *53*
6   Given the historical model of women who were active outside the   *54*
home in building America, it is really not surprising that American   *55*
women are working to reestablish their strong role in American   *56*
life.   *57*

Reading Clue

10.1   What word in line 4 emphasizes a contrast in ideas?

Look at page 224 for the answer.

C. Scanning

DIRECTIONS: *Write the number of the paragraph where you find the following information.*

a. _____ the "baby boom"

b. _____ the Protestant religion

c. _____ parents, sisters, cousins

d. _____ the women's movement

e. _____ nontraditional roles

f. _____ variety of lifestyles

g. _____ vacuum cleaners

h. _____ in the 1940s

i. _____ moved to the suburbs

j. _____ more easily than men

D. Vocabulary

DIRECTIONS: *Look at the following pairs of words. Find the word on the left in the reading. Compare its meaning to the word(s) on the right. Are the words similar or different? Write similar or different on the line.*

lifestyle (1)	way of life	1.	s
divorced (2)	married	2.	d
attitude (6)	feeling	3.	s
couple (10)	two people	4.	s
uncivilized (13)	civilized	5.	d

share (14)	work together	6. _____ s _____
definite (20)	general	7. _____ d _____
hostile (23)	unfriendly	8. _____ s _____
positions (34)	jobs	9. _____ s _____
capabilities (35)	abilities	10. _____ s _____
model (38)	form	11. _____ s _____
division (40)	separation	12. _____ s _____
far apart (41)	close together	13. _____ d _____
contribute (44)	add	14. _____ s _____
satisfying (49)	enjoyable	15. _____ s _____

E. Reading Comprehension

DIRECTIONS: Circle the letter of the choice that best completes each sentence.

1. The independent attitude of American women is ____.

   a. new   b. apparent historically   c. isolated

2. American colonists were generally ____ when they came to the New World.

   a. old   b. established   c. young

3. In the nineteenth century, women's roles were ____ strong.

   a. sometimes   b. always   c. never

4. In the suburbs, women ____ a part of their husbands' working lives.

   a. were usually not   b. felt they were   c. shared

5. When early Americans traveled west, the extended family ____.

   a. was broken up   b. stayed together   c. became closer

6. After World War II, women felt ____.

   a. tired   b. capable of work   c. dependent

7. Technological development made life ____ for American women.

   a. easier   b. more satisfying   c. longer

8. In the 1800s, it was often easier for ____ among the immigrants to find jobs.

   a. young people   b. men   c. women

9. The Protestant religion ____ the role of women.

    a. definitely determined   b. did not determine   c. occasionally determined

10. Early American women were ____ to be nontraditional.

    a. influenced   b. free   c. established

Look Again

A. Vocabulary

DIRECTIONS: Circle the letter of the choice that best completes each sentence.

1. When there is little variety, people have ____ .

   a. no time   b. few choices   c. a lot of diversity

2. The student had a negative attitude about her work. She ____ .

   a. hated it   b. studied hard   c. tried a lot

3. A ____ is an example of a time-saver.

   a. watch   b. dishwasher   c. bed

4. There were no other people. The boy was ____ .

   a. undeveloped   b. social   c. alone

5. The young people felt that they needed no help from anyone. They were very ____ .

   a. influenced   b. independent   c. uncivilized

6. A residential area has ____ .

   a. stores   b. houses   c. businesses

7. I ____ difficulties in language when I traveled to the Soviet Union.

   a. encountered   b. established   c. contributed to

8. The young people tried hard. They showed a lot of ____ .

   a. effort   b. status   c. influence

9. I ____ ten dollars to the organization.

   a. reinforced   b. shared   c. contributed

10. We make the same salaries, but our ____ is not the same because you have the title of "director."

    a. status   b. sense   c. model

B. Reading Comprehension

DIRECTIONS: Circle the letter of the choice that best completes each sentence.

1. The author thinks that there are ____ for American women.

    a. few possibilities   b. many choices   c. sometimes jobs

2. American women have felt independent ____ .

    a. only recently   b. for several   c. since World War II
                                  hundred years

3. Traditions were ____ survival in this new land.

    a. as important as   b. less important than   c. only for

4. American women ____ west with their husbands.

    a. did not go   b. left   c. moved

5. In the nineteenth and twentieth centuries, ____ American women worked.

    a. some   b. all   c. no

6. The move to the suburbs took place in the ____ .

    a. 1700s   b. 1800s   c. 1900s

7. According to the author, life in the suburbs had a ____ effect on women.

    a. positive   b. negative   c. hostile

8. A ____ was absolutely necessary in the suburbs.

    a. business   b. car   c. baby boom

9. Technological developments gave women more ____ .

    a. time   b. satisfaction   c. hands

10. The author feels that the women's movement is ____ a strong role for women.

    a. reestablishing   b. working for   c. working against

C. Questions

DIRECTIONS: Answer the following questions.

1. What is an extended family?

2. How is life different for women without an extended family? (Use your own ideas to answer.)

3. Why did the children of early Americans grow up with examples of strong women around them?

4. How does the author feel that life in the suburbs affected women? Do you agree or disagree?

5. What is the women's movement? What is your opinion of it?

section 3

Contact a Point of View

A. Timed Reading

DIRECTIONS: Read the following point of view and answer the questions in four minutes.

Jane Brown has been married for twelve years. She has three children and lives in a suburb outside Columbus, Ohio. When her youngest child reached school age, Jane decided to go back to work. She felt that she should contribute to the household finances; her salary could make the difference between a financial struggle and a secure financial situation for her family. Jane also felt bored and frustrated in her role as a housewife and wanted to be more involved in life outside her home.

Jane was worried about her children's adjustment to this new situation, but she arranged for them to go stay with a woman nearby after school each afternoon. They seem to be happy with the arrangement. The problems seem to be between Jane and her husband, Bill.

When Jane was at home all day, she was able to clean the house, go grocery shopping, wash the clothes, take care of the children, and cook two or three meals each day. She was very busy, of course, but she succeeded in getting everything done. Now these same things need to be done, but Jane has only evenings and early mornings to do them.

Both Jane and Bill are tired when they arrive home at 6:00 P.M. Bill is accustomed to sitting down and reading the paper or watching TV until dinner is ready. This is exactly what Jane feels like doing, but someone has to fix dinner and Bill expects it to be Jane. Jane is becoming very angry at Bill's attitude. She feels that they should share the household jobs; Bill feels that everything should be the same as it was before Jane went back to work.

DIRECTIONS: *Read each of the following statements carefully to determine whether each is true, false, or impossible to know. Check the appropriate blank.*

	TRUE	FALSE	IMPOSSIBLE TO KNOW
1. Jane Brown lives in Columbus, Indiana.		✓	
2. Money was one of the reasons why Jane wanted to work.	✓		
3. Jane liked her life as a housewife.		✓	
4. Jane was married once before her marriage to Bill.			✓
5. Jane and Bill wake up at 6:00 A.M.			✓
6. Jane wants to relax now after work.	✓		
7. Jane is a secretary.			✓
8. They were rich before Jane went back to work.		✓	
9. Jane worked at some time before this.	✓		

	TRUE	FALSE	IMPOSSIBLE TO KNOW
10. Jane and Bill work in the same building.	_____	_____	___✓___

B. Vocabulary

DIRECTIONS: Circle the letter of the word(s) with the same meaning as the italicized word.

1. I can't *contribute* any time to your program, but I will be happy to help out with money.

   a. give   b. take   c. have

2. There was a *struggle* between the two children over the football.

   a. fight   b. value   c. plan

3. After they put the money in the bank, they were sure that it was *secure*.

   a. broken   b. safe   c. difficult

4. What an *adjustment* it is to move from Florida to Vermont in January!

   a. problem   b. exclusion   c. changing process

5. We were *tired* because we did not get very much sleep.

   a. exhausted   b. unhappy   c. forced

6. Her *salary* is very high in her new job.

   a. hours   b. status   c. pay

7. They are both very *active* in their school.

   a. different   b. involved   c. absent

8. They may change their plans because they are not happy with the *arrangement*.

   a. situation   b. problems   c. people

9. She was unhappy with her *role* as housewife.

   a. time   b. position   c. house

10. What were the *effects* of the decision she made?

    a. results   b. reasons   c. causes

C. Word Forms

DIRECTIONS: Choose the appropriate word form for each sentence. Is it a noun, adjective, or verb?

1. vary
   various
   variety

1. There is little _____ in my job.

2. social
   socialize
   society

2. I can't believe that you hate to _____.

3. tradition
   traditional

3. This program is quite _____.

4. industry
   industrial
   industrialize

4. Pittsburgh is an _____ city.

5. reside
   residence
   residential

5. The census states that three people _____ at that address.

6. change
   changeable

6. The weather here is _____.

7. religion
   religious

7. She seems like a _____ person.

8. care
   careful

8. Take _____. You might fall.

9. separate
   separable
   separation

9. I cannot _____ these two pages.

10. secure
   security

10. Financial _____ is important to some people.

D. Speaking

DIRECTIONS: Read the timed reading again. Work with another student and answer the following questions. When you are finished, compare your ideas for numbers 5 and 6 with the other students' ideas.

1. What are the problems for Jane Brown?

2. What are the problems for the children?

3. What are the problems for Bill?

4. What are Jane's responsibilities?

5. What are three (3) possible solutions for these problems?

6. What should Jane and Bill do?

E. Writing

DIRECTIONS: Copy the following paragraphs. Choose only one word or phrase from each box.

should—something is a good idea.	*I should get enough sleep.*
have to—something is necessary.	*I have to take an exam tomorrow.*
be supposed to—a law, rule, or agreement	*They are supposed to meet me here.*
	We aren't supposed to smoke in this room.

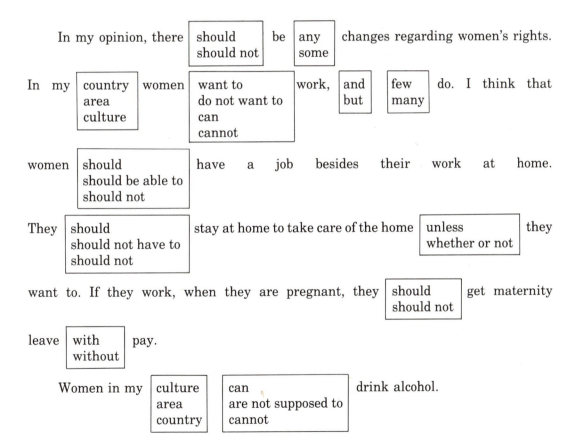

In my opinion, there | should / should not | be | any / some | changes regarding women's rights.

In my | country / area / culture | women | want to / do not want to / can / cannot | work, | and / but | few / many | do. I think that

women | should / should be able to / should not | have a job besides their work at home.

They | should / should not have to / should not | stay at home to take care of the home | unless / whether or not | they

want to. If they work, when they are pregnant, they | should / should not | get maternity

leave | with / without | pay.

Women in my | culture / area / country | can / are not supposed to / cannot | drink alcohol.

They | are not supposed to / can / cannot | smoke | either. / ,too. / ,however | They | can / are not supposed to / cannot | go out with

men alone on dates | and / but | they | never / are not supposed to / cannot / can | live with a man they are not

married to | although / and / . Therefore, | none / many / some | do. On the whole, women's behavior in

my | country / culture / area | is very | similar / different | from / to | women's behavior in the United States.

Look Back

A. Vocabulary

DIRECTIONS: Circle the letter of the choice that best completes each sentence.

1. The young man never questioned anything and did everything in the same way that his parents did. He was very ____.

   a. uncivilized   b. traditional   c. divorced

2. My ____ to the group was small, but they were happy to have help.

   a. contribution   b. establishment   c. solution

3. The ____ of cities in the West was important to early Americans.

   a. area   b. establishment   c. responsibility

4. An understanding of the past or a(n) ____ view is important for people today.

   a. ironic   b. Protestant   c. historical

5. The worker was good at his job and did it with ____.

   a. ease   b. factors   c. lifestyle

6. The army was losing the struggle against the enemy and needed ____, other groups of fighters and ammunition.

   a. society   b. exhaustion   c. reinforcements

7. She was very active in politics. Her ____ resulted in a government job.

   a. environment   b. involvement   c. advantage

8. The politician thanked her ____ for their help.

   a. supporters   b. factors   c. couples

9. I want to build a house, so I am looking for ____.

   a. land   b. environment   c. society

10. When should we go on our picnic? Time, weather, and hunger are the three ____ to think about.

   a. inventions   b. positions   c. factors

B. Matching

DIRECTIONS: Find the word or phrase in column B which has a similar meaning to a word in column A. Write the letter of that word or phrase next to the word in column A.

	A			**B**
1.	c	isolated	a.	job
2.	f	sense	b.	diversity
3.	g	active	c.	separated
4.	e	tired	d.	meet
5.	d	encounter	e.	exhausted
6.	a	position	f.	feeling
7.	b	variety	g.	involved
8.	i	secure	h.	only one
9.	h	alone	i.	safe
10.	j	arrange	j.	organize

chapter 11

Taxes, Taxes, and More Taxes

A First Look

A. Main Idea

DIRECTIONS: *Before you begin to read, look at these main ideas. There is one main idea for each paragraph. Write the number of the paragraph next to the main idea of that paragraph. Work <u>very quickly</u>. Do not read every word at this point.*

1. _____ everyone in agreement about taxes

2. _____ explanation of the national tax system

3. _____ the certainty of taxes

4. _____ three types of taxes in the United States

5. _____ urban taxes

6. _____ state tax revenues

B. Reading

DIRECTIONS: *Now read carefully.*

1   Americans often say that there are only two things a person can be sure of in life: death and taxes. Americans do not have a corner on the "death" market, but many people feel that the United States leads the world with the worst taxes.

2   Taxes consist of the money which people pay to support their government. There are generally three levels of government in the United States: federal, state, and city; therefore, there are three types of taxes.

3   Salaried people who earn more than a few thousand dollars must pay a certain percentage of their salaries to the federal (national) government. The percentage varies for individuals. It depends on their salaries. The federal government has a graduated income tax; that is, the percentage of the tax (14 to 70 percent)

increases as a person's income increases. With the high cost of taxes, people are not very happy on April 15, when the federal taxes are due. *14* *15* *16*

The second tax is for the state government: New York, California, North Dakota, or any of the other forty-seven states. Some states have an income tax similar to that of the federal government. Of course, the percentage for the state tax is lower. Other states have a sales tax, which is a percentage charged to any item which you buy in that state. For example, a person might want to buy a package of gum for twenty-five cents. If there is a sales tax of eight percent in that state, then the cost of the gum is twenty-seven cents. This figure includes the sales tax. Some states use income tax in addition to sales tax to raise their revenues. The state tax laws are diverse and confusing. *17* *18* *19* *20* *21* *22* *23* *24* *25* *26* *27*

The third tax is for the city. This tax comes in two forms: property tax (residents who own a home have to pay taxes on it) and excise tax, which is levied on vehicles in a city. The cities utilize these funds for education, police and fire departments, public works (including street repairs, water, and sanitation) and municipal buildings. *28* *29* *30* *31* *32* *33*

Since Americans pay such high taxes, they often feel that they are working one day each week just to pay their taxes. People always complain about taxes. They often protest that the government misuses their tax dollars. They say that it spends too much on useless and impractical programs. Although Americans have conflicting views on many issues—religious, racial, cultural, and political—they tend to agree on one subject: Taxes are too high. *34* *35* *36* *37* *38* *39* *40*

Reading Clue

11.1   Look at the last sentence of the article. Does the word *although* introduce an idea
(a) similar to the rest of the sentence?
(b) different from the rest of the sentence?
(c) as an example of the rest of the sentence?

Look at page 224 for the answer.

C. Scanning

DIRECTIONS: Write the number of the paragraph where you find the following information.

a. _____ tax similar to that of the federal government

b. _____ the percentage of federal taxes

c. _____ three types of taxes

d. _____ complain about taxes

e. _____ misuses taxes

f. _____ municipal buildings

g. _____ property tax

h. _____ tax levied on vehicles

i. _____ sales tax

j. _____ income tax in addition to sales tax

k. _____ two things a person can be sure of

l. _____ graduated income tax

D. Vocabulary

DIRECTIONS: Look at the following pairs of words. Find the word on the left in the reading. Compare its meaning to the word(s) on the right. Are the words similar or different? Write similar or different on the line.

consist of (5)	agree	1. _____
federal (7)	national	3. _____
types (8)	aspects	2. _____
varies (11)	remains the same	4. _____
graduated (12)	increasing	5. _____
due (16)	payable	6. _____
include (25)	keep out	7. _____
funds (31)	items	8. _____
repairs (32)	rebuilding	9. _____

municipal (32)	city or town	10. _____
complain (36)	enjoy	11. _____
protest (36)	disagree strongly	12. _____
misuse (36–37)	use carefully	13. _____
spend (37)	save	14. _____
impractical (38)	useful	15. _____
conflicting (38)	agreeing	16. _____
view (39)	opinion	17. _____
issue (39)	solution	18. _____
tend to (40)	seem to	19. _____
subject (40)	opinion	20. _____

E. Reading Comprehension

DIRECTIONS: Circle the letter of the choice that best completes each sentence.

1. In the United States, there are generally ____ basic types of taxes.

   a. two   b. three   c. four

2. A person must pay federal taxes if that person ____ .

   a. has a part-time job   b. lives in certain states   c. earns more than a few thousand dollars

3. Americans can be certain of only a few things. One is that ____ .

   a. the government misuses tax dollars   b. they will die   c. everyone pays taxes

4. Some states tax items which a person buys. This is a(n) ____ tax.

   a. income   b. sales   c. excise

5. State tax laws ____ .

   a. are fixed   b. are based on income   c. vary greatly

6. Cities get tax money from two different sources: homeowners and ____ .

   a. property   b. municipal employees   c. drivers

7. Americans think that they have to work one day out of every five to ____ .

   a. pay the government   b. relax   c. misuse their taxes

8. Each of the ____ states probably has individual tax laws.

   a. forty-seven   b. three   c. fifty

9. If a person who earns $20,000 pays 20 percent of it in federal taxes, a person who earns $30,000 pays ____ .

   a. 20 percent also   b. a lower percentage   c. more than $4,000

10. The author thinks that we can be certain about two things: ____ .

   a. useless and im-   b. taxes and death   c. sales tax and income
      practical programs   tax

Look Again

A. Vocabulary

DIRECTIONS: Circle the letter of the choice that best completes each sentence.

1. Taxes must be paid on a certain day. They are ____ on that day.

   a. sure   b. due   c. raised

2. A(n) ____ person earns an income.

   a. impractical   b. salaried   c. resident

3. The amount of income tax a person pays ____ his or her salary.

   a. depends on   b. earns   c. increases

4. People today are often careless, and we ____ our national resources.

   a. spend   b. complain about   c. misuse

5. You cannot agree. He has his ____ and you have yours.

   a. aspect   b. view   c. protest

6. The United States is a country of immigrants. There are many ____ of Americans.

   a. percentages   b. types   c. issues

7. How much tax did she ____ you?

   a. cost   b. charge   c. protest

8. When people from warm countries visit cold areas, they usually ____ about the weather.

   a. vary   b. complain   c. tend

9. It is ____ for a person who doesn't drive to buy a car.

   a. conflicting   b. impractical   c. confusing

10. Energy is one of the most important ____ of this century.

    a. issues   b. views   c. solutions

B. Reading Comprehension

DIRECTIONS: Circle the letter of the choice that best completes each sentence.

1. Property taxes pay for ____ .

    a. defense   b. education   c. vehicles

2. According to the author, Americans ____ agree about taxes.

    a. do   b. do not   c. cannot

3. Sales taxes are often part of the ____ system.

    a. city   b. state   c. national

4. There are ____ basic types of city taxes.

    a. three   b. two   c. four

5. The tax on a home is determined by ____ .

    a. its value   b. a percentage   c. the sales tax

6. There is a sales tax in ____ .

    a. all states   b. some states   c. fifty states

7. According to the author, Americans ____ agree about most issues.

    a. always   b. tend to   c. do not seem to

8. Religion and race relations are two very important ____ in the United States.

    a. points of view   b. conflicts   c. issues

9. State income tax is ____ .

    a. not graduated   b. a way to raise revenue   c. on every item

10. Americans do not have a "corner on the death market." This means that people ____ .

    a. die everywhere   b. do not die in other   c. consider death like a
                               places   market

C. Questions:

DIRECTIONS: Answer the following questions.

1. How many different types of taxes are there in the United States?

2. Who pays federal taxes in the United States?

3. What percentage of their salaries do Americans pay in taxes?

4. How do states raise their revenues?

5. How do cities and towns get their taxes?

6. How do Americans feel about taxes?

Contact a Point of View

A. Timed Reading

DIRECTIONS: Read the following point of view and answer the questions in four minutes.

Some people have all the luck. Here I am, a family man with three small children. I work hard for everything I have: a nice car, a house in the suburbs, and other conveniences. Lately, on TV, I've seen groups of people on welfare who complain that they can't get by on their incomes. How do you think I feel? People on welfare never work and have seven or eight children. Who pays the bills? I do. About 25 percent of my salary goes to taxes: the federal and the state taxes. Then, of course, there is the property tax on the house and the excise tax on the car. I've had it with taxes. Besides, the rate of inflation is increasing daily. It really angers me that I can't have the kind of life I deserve—the kind of life that I have worked for.

The President says that these are hard times and that we should not spend so much money, and then the defense budget goes up. The local politicians say that they need more money for highway repairs, and then they vote a salary increase for themselves. The town selectmen say we need a new elementary school. We just can't afford it. Who helps me when the kids need new sneakers? No one. People used to say that the rich get richer and the poor get poorer. Now I am beginning to think that the people in the middle class are the real losers.

DIRECTIONS: *Read each of the following statements carefully to determine whether each is true, false, or impossible to know. Check the appropriate blank.*

	TRUE	FALSE	IMPOSSIBLE TO KNOW
1. This man lives in the city.	_____	_____	_____
2. Twenty-five percent of his salary goes to taxes.	_____	_____	_____
3. He has three older children.	_____	_____	_____
4. He pays taxes on his home.	_____	_____	_____
5. Money for education comes from the state.	_____	_____	_____
6. He is on welfare.	_____	_____	_____
7. He is from the upper class.	_____	_____	_____
8. He thinks that the middle class is lucky.	_____	_____	_____
9. Local politicians have high salaries.	_____	_____	_____
10. The President wants people to conserve.	_____	_____	_____

B. Vocabulary

DIRECTIONS: *Circle the letter of the word(s) with the same meaning as the italicized word(s).*

1. I can't have the kind of life I *deserve*.

   a. should have   b. can have   c. had

2. It *angers* him that he can't have an easy life.

   a. confuses　　　　　　　b. upsets　　　　　　　　c. worries

3. We should not *complain* about taxes. They are necessary.

   a. feel unhappy　　　　　b. say bad things　　　　c. care

4. The defense budget *goes up* yearly.

   a. decreases　　　　　　b. increases　　　　　　　c. changes

5. These are some of our *local* politicians.

   a. far away　　　　　　　b. misplaced　　　　　　c. from the area

6. A large percentage of the national budget is for *defense*.

   a. politicians　　　　　b. the military　　　　　c. the presidency

7. People in the middle class are the real *losers*.

   a. people who don't gain　　b. people who don't lose　　c. people who complain

8. There are many *conveniences* in American homes.

   a. interesting things　　　b. affordable objects　　c. helpful things

C. Word Forms

DIRECTIONS: *Read the following information about* <u>adverbs</u> *and* <u>adjectives</u> *and then complete the exercises. Decide if the italicized words in the sentences are adverbs or adjectives.*

(noun)

<u>Adjectives</u> explain <u>nouns</u> more clearly:　He is a <u>slow</u> speaker.

(verb)

<u>Adverbs</u> explain <u>verbs</u> more clearly:　He speaks <u>slowly</u>.

<u>Adverbs</u> can also explain <u>adjectives</u> or other <u>adverbs</u> more clearly:

(adverb)　　　　　(adjective)

She speaks <u>very</u>　slowly . She is a <u>very</u>　　slow　speaker.

	ADVERB	ADJECTIVE
1. She is always *independent*.	_____	_____
2. His ideas are *practically* impossible.	_____	_____
3. She arrives late *consistently*.	_____	_____

	ADVERB	ADJECTIVE
4. Those cars are really *fast*.	_____	_____
5. He drives *fast*.	_____	_____
6. They are a *typical* American family.	_____	_____
7. I *always* get up late.	_____	_____
8. *Lately*, I have been thinking about a vacation.	_____	_____
9. The style of her letter was very *formal*.	_____	_____
10. *Naturally*, she doesn't want to give up her job.	_____	_____

D. Speaking

DIRECTIONS: What do you think about taxes? Answer the following questions and share your ideas with a classmate or the class.

1. Should people pay taxes?

2. Which people should pay taxes? Only the rich? The poor? The middle class?

3. What percentage of income should be for taxes?

4. Should taxes be graduated?

If and when taxes are necessary to support the government, how should they be used? Number the following from 1 to 12. Number 1 is the most important and number 12 is the least important. What are your opinions?

_____ defense

_____ welfare

_____ unemployment compensation

_____ social security

_____ education

_____ old-age homes

_____ health care

_____ day-care centers*

_____ roads and highways

_____ public transportation

_____ energy research

_____ pollution control

E. Writing

DIRECTIONS: *Complete the following sentences, which contain the word although. Remember that although introduces a contrasting idea. If the clause with although is at the beginning of the sentence, put a comma after that part of the sentence. If it is in the second part of the sentence, no comma is necessary. Complete the sentences as you wish.*

For example: Although he was very intelligent,

he never did any work.

1. Although he studied very hard last semester _____

_____.

2. Although the television is a very important factor in American life _____

_____.

3. We had the party although _____.

4. Although he had no money in his bank account _____

_____.

5. Although I enjoy my job _____.

* Day-care centers are places where children can stay when their parents are working. These centers are usually for children not old enough for school or for older children after school hours.

6. Although she likes apartment living _____

   _____ .

7. He is buying a new car although _____

   _____ .

8. Although _____
   he is a very old friend of mine.

9. Although _____
   sometimes I get homesick.

10. Although _____
    I often feel that I'll never learn English.

Look Back

A. Vocabulary

DIRECTIONS: Circle the letter of the choice that best completes each sentence.

1. He has many strong ideas. He is very ____ .

   a. opinionated   b. changeable   c. impractical

2. We cannot decide; we ____ about everything.

   a. raise   b. avoid   c. disagree

3. Food is not ____ in some states.

   a. graduated   b. taxable   c. variable

4. My watch is very ____ .

   a. valuable   b. conflicting   c. solvable

5. He gave me the wrong directions. I was ____ .

   a. impractical   b. misinformed   c. directed

6. My telephone bill is ____ tomorrow.

   a. paid   b. due   c. differentiated

7. She ____ happy, but I'm not sure.

   a. tends to be   b. certainly is   c. seems

8. He is a good father; he is very ____ his children.

   a. supportive of   b. dependent on   c. uncertain of

9. The federal government ____ many educational programs.

   a. consists of   b. funds   c. spends

10. The students were very dissatisfied. We listened to their ____ .

    a. experiences   b. complaints   c. models

B. Matching

DIRECTIONS: *Find the word or phrase in column B which has a similar meaning to a word or phrase in column A. Write the letter of that word or phrase next to the word or phrase in column A.*

A	B
1. _____ impractical	a. property
2. _____ possessions	b. complain
3. _____ seem to	c. useless
4. _____ protest	d. utilize
5. _____ comprise	e. extra
6. _____ additional	f. appear to
7. _____ national	g. include
8. _____ kind	h. federal
9. _____ repair	i. type
10. _____ use	j. fix

Answer Key
Section 1: **A.** 1. 6 2. 3 3. 1 4. 2 5. 5 6. 4 **C.** a. 4 b. 3 c. 2 d. 6 e. 6 f. 5 g. 5 h. 5 i. 4 j. 4 k. 1 l. 3 **D.** 1. different 2. similar 3. similar 4. different 5. similar 6. similar 7. different 8. different 9. similar 10. similar 11. different 12. similar 13. different 14. different 15. different 16. different 17. similar 18. different 19. similar 20. different **E.** 1. b 2. c 3. b 4. b 5. c 6. c 7. a 8. c 9. c 10. b
Section 2: **A.** 1. b 2. b 3. a 4. c 5. b 6. b 7. b 8. b 9. b 10. a **B.** 1. b 2. a 3. b 4. b 5. a 6. b 7. c 8. c 9. b 10. a
Section 3: **A.** 1. F 2. T 3. F 4. T 5. F 6. F 7. F 8. F 9. ITK 10. T **B.** 1. a 2. b 3. b 4. b 5. c 6. b 7. a 8. c **C.** 1. adjective 2. adverb 3. adverb 4. adjective 5. adverb 6. adjective 7. adverb 8. adverb 9. adjective 10. adverb
Section 4: **A.** 1. a 2. c 3. b 4. a 5. b 6. b 7. c 8. a 9. b 10. b **B.** 1. c 2. a 3. f 4. b 5. g 6. e 7. h 8. i 9. j 10. d

chapter 12

The Energy Crisis

section 1 ————————————————————

A First Look

A. Main Idea

DIRECTIONS: *Before you begin to read, look at these main ideas. There is one main idea for each paragraph. Write the number of the paragraph next to the main idea of that paragraph. Work very quickly. Do not read every word at this point.*

1. _____ immediate energy solutions

2. _____ solutions from scientists

3. _____ U.S. dependency on fuel

4. _____ domestic fuel sources

5. _____ benefits of solar power

B. Reading

DIRECTIONS: *Now read carefully.*

1
    The United States is a country dependent on fuel: We have to   *1*
heat our homes, drive our cars, and run our factories. We have a   *2*
great need for energy because of our fast-paced lifestyle. Once we   *3*
thought that there was no end to fuel; now we realize that supplies   *4*
are very limited, particularly here in the United States. Prices for   *5*
foreign oil are increasing daily, and someday we may not be able   *6*
to get oil, because of difficult world politics, even if we can afford   *7*
it. We must find a solution to our dependence on foreign energy; we   *8*
must find usable energy in our own nation.   *9*

2
    In addition to petroleum, we have other domestic sources of   *10*
energy: natural gas, coal, and wood. Natural gas can offer some   *11*
relief from insufficient oil supplies. Like oil, however, natural gas   *12*
is limited and in time will run out. Coal is an abundant domestic   *13*
source of energy, but the use of coal causes increased pollution.   *14*
Wood is another source of energy, but it is expensive, and the cutting   *15*

A First Look 177

of large forest areas also causes environmental problems, such as   16
mud slides and erosion.   17

3   Recently scientists have been developing and perfecting other   18
sources of energy: nuclear or atomic power, solar (sun) power, and   19
synthetic (man-made) fuels. Nuclear power can offer some assis-   20
tance, but fear of contamination limits its use. The Three Mile Island   21
accident in Pennsylvania in 1979, when atomic waste material es-   22
caped into the atmosphere, limited power plant construction greatly.   23
In addition, scientists are doing research to discover other sources   24
of fuel. In fact, some scientists have added alcohol to gasoline to   25
conserve fuel. Unfortunately, this research is still in the develop-   26
mental stage.   27

The sun, from which nearly all energy derives, is another so-   28
lution to the energy crisis. Solar power is growing rapidly in pop-   29
ularity. All other fuels will run out after a period of years; the sun's   30
power is limitless. Although burning any fuel—oil, coal, or wood—   31
causes pollution, solar energy does not. Furthermore, no nation on   32
4   earth has a corner on the solar market; that is, no country has   33
control over the sun. Although solar energy is increasing in popu-   34
larity, it is still impractical and very expensive, and therefore not   35
widely used.   36

One immediate and viable (practical) solution to the problem   37
is conservation. We now have federal regulations limiting the winter   38
temperature in public buildings to 65 degrees. Homeowners are   39
insulating their houses to prevent heat loss, and in general, people   40
are keeping "cool." Drivers are taking public transportation—buses,   41
trains, and subways—or joining car pools (groups of people who   42
5   drive to work together). Even Detroit, the automobile capital, is   43
adjusting to the change. Small cars are now commonplace on Amer-   44
ican highways. Americans are looking for new ways to solve the   45
energy crisis. We are putting our heads together and our sweaters   46
on to find solutions.   47

Reading Clue

12.1   Do the expressions *in addition to* in line 10 and
furthermore in line 32
(a) introduce more ideas?
(b) explain the same idea?
(c) introduce a contrast (a different idea)?
Look at page 224 for the answer.

C. Scanning

DIRECTIONS: Write the number of the paragraph where you find the following information.

a. _____ fast-paced lifestyle

b. _____ prices for foreign oil

c. _____ not widely used

d. _____ control over the sun

e. _____ atomic waste material

f. _____ our sweaters on

g. _____ insulating

h. _____ car pools

i. _____ environmental problems, such as erosion

j. _____ research to discover other fuels

D. Vocabulary

DIRECTIONS: Look at the following pairs of words. Find the word on the left in the reading. Compare its meaning to the word(s) on the right. Are the words similar or different? Write _similar_ or _different_ on the line.

realize (4)	understand	1. _____
particularly (5)	in general	2. _____
domestic (10)	foreign	3. _____
sources (10)	supplies	4. _____
insufficient (12)	limited	5. _____
run out (13)	use completely	6. _____
abundant (13)	limited	7. _____
recently (18)	lately	8. _____
nuclear (19)	atomic	9. _____
synthetic (20)	natural	10. _____
contamination (21)	pollution	11. _____

in addition (24)	furthermore	12. _____
derive from (28)	come from	13. _____
crisis (28)	problem	14. _____
immediate (37)	future	15. _____
viable (37)	impractical	16. _____
conservation (38)	saving	17. _____
regulations (38)	rules	18. _____
insulate (40)	keep cool or hot	19. _____
solution (47)	problem	20. _____

E. Reading Comprehension

DIRECTIONS: Circle the letter of the choice that best completes each sentence.

1. _____ is not a cause of pollution.

   a. Nuclear power   b. Coal   c. Solar power

2. The author mentions *three* different problems with oil: It is expensive, it is limited, and _____.

   a. it is a usable source of energy   b. we cannot afford it   c. we may not be able to buy it because of politics

3. "Heating our homes, driving our cars, and running our factories" are examples of _____.

   a. limitless fuel supplies   b. fast-paced lifestyles   c. dependency on fuel

4. Solar power is _____.

   a. practical   b. widely used   c. growing in popularity

5. "Limiting the winter temperature . . . to 65 degrees" is an example of _____.

   a. contamination   b. conservation   c. insulation

6. The greatest fear with nuclear power is _____.

   a. expense   b. construction   c. pollution

7. There are two aspects to the crisis in paragraph 1: We must find and use domestic energy and _____.

   a. agree to pay high prices   b. decrease our need for fuel from other nations   c. increase domestic fuel use

8. Natural gas and oil are similar because they both ____ .

   a. will run out

   b. are limitless

   c. can offer some relief to insufficient fuel supplies

9. Coal and wood are alike because they both ____ .

   a. are expensive

   b. cause environmental problems

   c. are practical solutions

10. ____ limited the construction of atomic power plants.

   a. Research

   b. An accident

   c. Popularity

Look Again

A. Vocabulary

DIRECTIONS: Circle the letter of the choice that best completes each sentence.

1. That is a fine restaurant, but get there early. They ____ food at 9:00 P.M.

    a. conserve   b. insulate   c. run out of

2. I have to go to the library to do some ____.

    a. research   b. sources   c. transportation

3. I am very homesick, ____ on weekends.

    a. particularly   b. in general   c. furthermore

4. I have a really difficult problem. Can you help me ____ it?

    a. cause   b. solve   c. realize

5. He is ____ on his father since he doesn't have a job.

    a. viable   b. usable   c. dependent

6. Fresh fruit is ____ in the summer.

    a. abundant   b. insufficient   c. synthetic

7. This medicine provides ____ relief; you will feel better in a few minutes.

    a. natural   b. general   c. immediate

8. The United States has many international conflicts, in addition to the ____ ones.

    a. foreign   b. synthetic   c. domestic

9. According to the author, ____ is a quick solution to the present energy crisis.

    a. conservation   b. regulation   c. dependence

10. The word *synthetic* ____ from Greek.

    a. researches   b. derives   c. conserves

B. Reading Comprehension

DIRECTIONS: Circle the letter of the choice that best completes each sentence.

1. In the last paragraph, the author's attitude toward the energy crisis is ____ .

   a. positive   b. negative   c. neutral

2. "Much of the energy research is in the developmental stage" means that scientists are ____ .

   a. developing stages of energy
   b. at the beginning of their research
   c. developing energy stages

3. In paragraph 3, the author mentions Three Mile Island to ____ .

   a. explain the lack of construction
   b. show about developmental research
   c. demonstrate synthetic fuels

4. Solar energy ____ .

   a. causes pollution and will run out
   b. is impractical and decreasing in popularity
   c. is abundant but not widely used

5. Nuclear power causes ____ .

   a. contamination   b. conservation   c. construction

6. What happens in ____ is an important factor in oil conservation.

   a. Pennsylvania   b. forest areas   c. Detroit

7. World politics change so rapidly that we *may* not be able to ____ .

   a. afford oil   b. buy oil   c. find solutions

8. Mud slides and erosion are the results of ____ .

   a. environment   b. cutting trees   c. increasing forest areas

9. ____ is one way of fighting the energy crisis.

   a. Taking the bus
   b. Driving around with friends
   c. Taking a taxi

10. Once, Americans thought that fuel ____ .

    a. was limited   b. would never run out   c. would not be available

C. Questions

DIRECTIONS: Answer the following questions.

1. What are the two responses to the energy crisis stated in paragraph 1?

2. Give some examples of fuel sources and explain why they are not viable solutions to the energy crisis.

3. Give three benefits of solar power and three benefits of atomic power.

4. What is your country doing to increase fuel sources?

5. What are some examples of conservation that you have seen people practicing?

section 3

Contact a Point of View

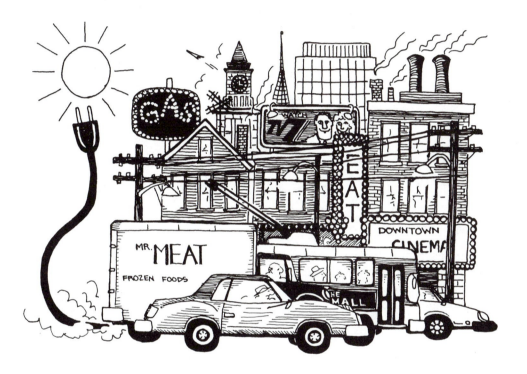

A. Timed Reading

> *DIRECTIONS: Read the following point of view and answer the questions in four minutes.*

"No nukes. No nukes." The demonstrators want to stop construction of nuclear power plants—nukes. Since the Three Mile Island accident in the late 1970s, we have begun to realize that there is a great risk with atomic power. We are really not sure how to control nuclear power. The nuclear reaction produces highly contaminated waste material which can pollute both the water and land around a power plant. The contaminated gas can also pollute huge areas of space. Scientists do not even know the long-term effects contamination has on people. They can only guess. We cannot afford to guess with human life.

People complain that we don't have enough power, that we have to find other sources. I think that the government has to do more research on the benefits of solar power. Solar power is expensive, but if the government supports solar development, we will see a different point of view from individuals and from industry. Solar power is safe, nonpolluting, and abundant. It is a source of energy that will protect jobs and protect human beings from certain suicide. To protect ourselves, to protect those we love, and to protect our very existence, we must control nuclear power plant construction. Remember the slogan: "Nuclear destroys, solar employs."

DIRECTIONS: *Read each of the following statements carefully to determine whether each is true, false, or impossible to know. Check the appropriate blank.*

	TRUE	FALSE	IMPOSSIBLE TO KNOW
1. A nuke is an atomic power plant.	_____	_____	_____
2. Three Mile Island happened in the early 1970s.	_____	_____	_____
3. Nuclear reactions produce waste material.	_____	_____	_____
4. This person thinks that solar energy is bad.	_____	_____	_____
5. Solar energy is nonpolluting.	_____	_____	_____
6. Solar power is expensive.	_____	_____	_____
7. Nuclear waste only contaminates the air.	_____	_____	_____
8. Solar energy is more expensive than nuclear energy.	_____	_____	_____
9. This person wants more atomic energy research.	_____	_____	_____
10. With government support, atomic power will be successful.	_____	_____	_____

B. Vocabulary

DIRECTIONS: Fill in the blanks in the following sentences with vocabulary from the reading.

1. site/realize/risk

   Many people do not _____ the _____

   they are taking when they visit a nuclear power plant _____ .

2. guess/slogan

   Can you _____ the advertising _____

   for that product?

3. highly/waste/produce

   Atomic reactions _____ dangerous and _____

   toxic _____ .

C. Word Forms

DIRECTIONS: Choose the appropriate word form for each sentence. Is it an adjective or an adverb?

	ADJECTIVE	ADVERB
	natural	naturally
	formal	formally

1. careful
   carefully

2. traditional
   traditionally

3. essential
   essentially

4. serious
   seriously

5. perfect
   perfectly

6. social
   socially

1. He spoke _____ about the problem.

2. My father dresses very _____ .

3. It is _____ to study all aspects of the problem.

4. She is _____ about her work.

5. That design is _____ beautiful.

6. He is nervous _____ .

7. cultural
   culturally

7. Lifestyles vary _____ .

8. vast
   vastly

8. Our opinions are _____ different.

9. minimal
   minimally

9. That change is _____ .

10. ironic
    ironically

10. That play was extremely _____ .

D. Speaking

The conflict between solar energy and nuclear energy is very important these days. What are the negative and positive aspects of each?

DIRECTIONS: Discuss or debate the pros and cons of nuclear energy and solar energy. Do you know other alternatives to the energy crisis?

E. Writing

DIRECTIONS: After you have debated the issue of energy, break into groups of three or four to write the statement of your position. This is a group writing assignment.

Look Back

A. Vocabulary

DIRECTIONS: Circle the letter of the choice that best completes each sentence.

1. I'll be there at 3:00 P.M. Don't worry. You can ____ on me.

   a. depend b. join c. put

2. Our natural resources include gas, coal, and wood ____ oil.

   a. in addition to b. furthermore c. in particular

3. Some energy ____ the sun.

   a. solves b. conserves c. derives from

4. Even oil will __ someday.

   a. complete b. limit c. run out

5. Coal ____ pollution.

   a. causes b. prevents c. derives

6. Natural gas is an example of ____ .

   a. energy b. a fuel c. a source

7. Three months of study is ____ to learn a language.

   a. supportive b. conservative c. insufficient

8. World politics may prevent us from getting oil; ____ we must find other sources.

   a. therefore, b. but c. furthermore,

9. Let's ____ out heads together and decide.

   a. join b. take c. put

10. Large boats ____ oil across the ocean.

    a. insulate b. transport c. support

B. Matching

DIRECTIONS: Find the word or phrase in column B which has a similar meaning to a word or phrase in column A. Write the letter of that word or phrase next to the word or phrase in column A.

	A		B
1. _____	in general	a.	speedy
2. _____	fast-paced	b.	relief
3. _____	prevent	c.	solve
4. _____	assistance	d.	limitless
5. _____	conserve	e.	synthetic
6. _____	viable	f.	furthermore
7. _____	contaminated	g.	derive from
8. _____	abundant	h.	for the most part
9. _____	additionally	i.	realize
10. _____	answer	j.	stop
11. _____	come from	k.	save
12. _____	understand	l.	practical
13. _____	man-made	m.	polluted

chapter 13

Freedom of Religion

A First Look

A. Main Idea

DIRECTIONS: Before you begin to read, look at these main ideas. There is one main idea for each paragraph. Write the number of the paragraph next to the main idea of that paragraph. Work very quickly. Do not read every word at this point.

1. _____ general description of Christianity

2. _____ the Jewish religion

3. _____ the Protestant church

4. _____ historical background for freedom of religion

5. _____ the Roman Catholic church

6. _____ traditional feelings about non-Protestant beliefs

7. _____ deemphasis on religion

B. Reading

DIRECTIONS: Now read carefully.

1

    The first immigrants who came to New England in the 1600s   *1*
left their own countries for religious reasons. They had religious   *2*
beliefs different from the accepted beliefs of their country; they   *3*
wanted to live in a place where they could be free to have their own   *4*
beliefs. When they came to establish new communities in the New   *5*
World, they decided that there would be no official religion. When   *6*
this new country gained its independence from Britain in 1776, the   *7*
separation of church and government was one of the basic laws for   *8*
the United States. This absence of an official national religion and   *9*
the resultant freedom to believe in whatever one wants has attracted   *10*
many new immigrants. In the United States, there are examples of   *11*

every kind of world religion—Buddhist, Islamic, Baha'i, to name *12*
only a few. But most of the people in the United States fall into one *13*
of two categories—Christian or Jewish. *14*

2   The majority of people in the United States were raised as *15*
Christians. Quite simply, Christian means believing in Christ, or *16*
Jesus. Christians celebrate Christmas, the birth of Christ, and *17*
Easter, the time of Jesus's death. They think of Sunday as a holy *18*
day and worship in churches. In the United States, Christianity can *19*
be divided into two major groups: Roman Catholicism and *20*
Protestantism. *21*

3   As its name suggests, the Roman Catholic church is based in *22*
Rome. It is centered around the authority of one man, the Pope, who *23*
is the head of the Roman Catholic church throughout the world. *24*
There is a hierarchy of authority and responsibility beginning with *25*
the Pope in Rome and ending with the priests who are the heads *26*
of the churches in individual neighborhoods and communities. *27*

4   Protestant refers to any Christian church which is not Roman *28*
Catholic. As its name suggests, the Protestant church began as a *29*
protest against another church: the Roman Catholic church. Prot- *30*
estant is a very general term; it includes many different church *31*
groups, such as Episcopalian, Presbyterian, Lutheran, Mormon, *32*
Baptist, and many more. The majority of people in the United States *33*
have Protestant backgrounds. However, since there are so many *34*
Protestant churches, each with its own traditions, people who are *35*
Protestants do not really share similar religious experiences. As *36*
opposed to the Roman Catholic church in which there is a lot of *37*
central control, Protestant churches are generally more autono- *38*
mous, with more control and authority on a local level. *39*

5   Jews and Christians share many of the same basic principles *40*
and beliefs. They both believe in the existence of one God. But *41*
whereas Christians believe in Christ, a representation of God on *42*
earth, Jews do not believe that God has come to earth in any form. *43*
Jewish people celebrate a weekly holy day from Friday evening to *44*
Saturday evening and worship in synagogues. The head of a syn- *45*
agogue is called a rabbi. Many Jewish people came to the United *46*
States in the first half of the twentieth century because of religious *47*
intolerance in their own countries. *48*

6   Although freedom of religion is an important concept in the *49*
United States, religious intolerance sometimes occurs. Because the *50*
majority of early Americans were Protestant, there has sometimes *51*
been discrimination against new immigrants, such as the Irish and *52*
Italians, who were Roman Catholic. Protestants were reluctant to *53*
share their traditional power with members of other churches or *54*

religions. The year 1960 marked a breakthrough in the religious   55
tolerance of the country when John F. Kennedy, a Roman Catholic,   56
became the first nonProtestant President of the United States.   57

7

The second half of the twentieth century has seen a decline in   58
the strength of traditional religion in the United States. It is prob-   59
ably to be expected that in a society that accepts so many different   60
religions, religion would be deemphasized. Intermarriage is now   61
common and fewer people think about traditional religious beliefs.   62

Reading Clues

13.1 Find a word or phrase in lines 36–37 and a word
      in line 42 which show contrast.
      What are the words or phrases?

Look at page 224 for the answer.

13.2 What does *since* in line 34 introduce?
      (a) a contrast
      (b) an example
      (c) a reason

Look at page 224 for the answer.

C. Scanning

DIRECTIONS: Write the number of the paragraph where you find the following information.

a. _____ the Pope

b. _____ Irish and Italians

c. _____ first half of the twentieth century

d. _____ 1776

e. _____ Baha'i

f. _____ authority on a local level

g. _____ Christmas, the birth of Christ

h. _____ synagogues

i. _____ separation of church and government

j. _____ intermarriage now common

D. Vocabulary

DIRECTIONS: Look at the following pairs of words. Find the word on the left in the reading.
Compare its meaning to the word(s) on the right. Are the words similar or different?
Write *similar* or *different* on the line.

accepted (3)	traditional	1. _____
official (6)	unofficial	2. _____
independence (7)	freedom	3. _____
separation (8)	division	4. _____
basic (8)	additional	5. _____
attracted (10)	interested	6. _____
categories (14)	groups	7. _____
majority (15)	minority	8. _____
birth (17)	death (18)	9. _____
based (22)	centered	10. _____
hierarchy (25)	power structure	11. _____
background (34)	future	12. _____
intolerance (48)	tolerance	13. _____
occurs (50)	happens	14. _____
reluctant (53)	unwilling	15. _____

E. Reading Comprehension

DIRECTIONS: Circle the letter of the choice that best completes each sentence.

1. Most people in the United States have ____ backgrounds.

    a. Protestant   b. Roman Catholic   c. Jewish

2. The early Americans were ____ .

    a. Protestant   b. Roman Catholic   c. Jewish

3. Many Jewish people came to the United States ____ .

   a. in the 1600s   b. before 1950   c. in the 1950s

4. According to the author, ____ is more hierarchical than other religions.

   a. the Jewish religion   b. Protestantism   c. Roman Catholicism

5. According to the author, in the second half of the twentieth century, traditional religion has ____ power.

   a. gained   b. lost   c. no

6. According to the author, there ____ religious discrimination in the United States.

   a. is now no   b. has sometimes been   c. never used to be

7. Protestants belong to ____ .

   a. many different churches   b. the Roman Catholic church   c. similar churches

8. The United States has ____ religion.

   a. an official   b. no   c. no official

9. The ____ people came to the United States because of its religious freedom.

   a. Jewish   b. Irish   c. Buddhist

10. In the Protestant church, there is ____ control on the local level.

   a. no   b. a lot of   c. rarely

Look Again

A. Vocabulary

DIRECTIONS: Circle the letter of the choice that best completes each sentence.

1. Both churches and synagogues are places where people ____ .

   a. believe   b. worship   c. attract

2. Most large organizations have a ____ of power and authority.

   a. hierarchy   b. reluctance   c. reason

3. My friend is the ____ of the department. She is the supervisor.

   a. head   b. representation   c. priest

4. A director in a company has the ____ to make decisions.

   a. hierarchy   b. persecution   c. authority

5. This painting is an example of realism. It is a ____ of a rainstorm.

   a. concept   b. representation   c. principle

6. He never thinks about his religious ____ .

   a. level   b. head   c. beliefs

7. The mayor of a city is not involved in the federal government. The mayor is in ____ government.

   a. national   b. individual   c. local

8. The president's wife was the ____ head of the company.

   a. unofficial   b. attracted   c. raised

9. The town, not the state, had control of its own policies. The town was ____ .

   a. autonomous   b. tolerant   c. centered

10. We decided not to go running ____ it was raining out.

    a. throughout   b. since   c. as opposed to

B. Reading Comprehension

DIRECTIONS: Circle the letter of the choice that best completes each sentence.

1. According to the author, it is ____ for a Christian to marry a Jew now in the United States.

   a. unusual   b. common   c. traditional

2. According to the author, traditional religion is ____ important now as (than) it was in the early 1900s.

   a. less   b. as   c. more

3. One difference between the Protestant church and the Roman Catholic church is ____.

   a. belief in Christ   b. local autonomy   c. celebration of Christmas

4. The United States separated from England in ____.

   a. 1492   b. the 1600s   c. the 1700s

5. Most people in the United States have ____ backgrounds.

   a. Jewish   b. Roman Catholic   c. Protestant

6. Episcopal is a ____ church.

   a. Jewish   b. Roman Catholic   c. Protestant

7. In paragraph 5, the author states that one difference between Jews and Christians is belief in ____.

   a. one God   b. God on earth   c. a holy day each week

8. Different religious beliefs are generally ____ in the United States.

   a. accepted   b. persecuted   c. discriminated against

9. Religious discrimination ____ happened between Roman Catholics and Protestants in the United States.

   a. always   b. sometimes   c. never

10. The Pope is the head of all ____.

    a. Christians   b. Italians   c. Roman Catholics

C. Questions

DIRECTIONS: Answer the following questions.

1. What is one of the basic laws in the United States which is mentioned in the reading?

2. Why is there no official religion in the United States?

3. What are the two subdivisions of Christianity in the United States?

4. Why did many Jews come to the United States?

5. Has religious intolerance occurred in the United States? Give one example.

Contact a Point of View

A. Timed Reading

DIRECTIONS: Read the following point of view and answer the questions in four minutes.

Alice Shapen is a member of a religious group which believes in the establishment of a universal religion, one which will join all the religions of the world into one. She joined this group three years ago when she was eighteen and a freshman in college. She often thinks about how lonely she was before she met the people she now lives with who came up to her on the street and just began talking to her for no apparent reason. Alice was happy to spend time with them because they were so friendly. Now she is one of the ones who goes out to try to meet new people and bring them back to join her friends.

Alice's parents do not share her feelings about the religious group that she belongs to. In their opinion this group took advantage of Alice's loneliness and, essentially, kidnapped her. They think that the group somehow "brainwashed" their daughter. She is not the same person they used to know and never visits them. She spends all her time with members of the religious group, either working in a business which they own or trying to bring new members into the group.

The Shapens have tried unsuccessfully to convince Alice to leave the group. They feel that this group has ruined their daughter's life and that she is no longer a free person. They are considering taking an action which other parents of people in this group have done, that is, kidnapping their child back from the group. They want to hire someone to get Alice away from the group and then "deprogram" her, to make her the Alice they used to know. They realize that this is a dangerous plan; Alice may not be able to stay away from the group, and the group has sometimes brought criminal charges against parents who paid to have their children kidnapped. They feel, however, that this is their only chance to save Alice.

DIRECTIONS: *Read each of the following statements carefully to determine whether each is true, false, or impossible to know. Check the appropriate blank.*

	TRUE	FALSE	IMPOSSIBLE TO KNOW
1. Alice is twenty-one.	_____	_____	_____
2. Alice was a Christian until she met the people in this religious group.	_____	_____	_____
3. Alice does not work now.	_____	_____	_____
4. Alice was "brainwashed."	_____	_____	_____
5. The Shapens are the only parents to think about kidnapping someone from this group.	_____	_____	_____
6. It may be illegal to kidnap your own child.	_____	_____	_____
7. Alice does not visit her parents now.	_____	_____	_____

	TRUE	FALSE	IMPOSSIBLE TO KNOW
8. The Shapens are religious people.	_____	_____	_____
9. The Shapens want someone to kidnap Alice.	_____	_____	_____
10. Alice lives with other members of the group.	_____	_____	_____

B. Vocabulary

DIRECTIONS: Circle the letter of the word(s) with the same meaning as the italicized word.

1. Poverty is a *universal* problem.

   a. large   b. depressing   c. worldwide

2. I want to *join* a tennis club.

   a. become a member of   b. pay for   c. be a member of

3. I can't *convince* you that you are wrong.

   a. tell   b. persuade   c. refuse

4. We tried *unsuccessfully* to start the car.

   a. hard   b. without result   c. for a long time

5. Their mistake was immediately *apparent*.

   a. obvious   b. fixed   c. hidden

6. I *considered* changing my profession.

   a. wanted to begin   b. tried   c. thought about

7. The dessert was *ruined*, so no one could eat it.

   a. destroyed   b. burnt   c. delicious

8. The politician *charged* his opponent with lying.

   a. demanded money   b. accused   c. called

9. The company can't *hire* me until July.

   a. pay   b. give a job to   c. use

10. I don't know how to *program* a computer.

    a. feed information to   b. start   c. use the information in

C. Word Forms

DIRECTIONS: *Choose the appropriate word form for each sentence. Is it a noun, adjective, adverb, or verb?*

general
generally
generalize
generalization

1. We _____ go home at about 5:30 P.M.

2. It is easy to _____ about things which are unfamiliar to you.

individual
individually
individualize
individualization

3. The teacher talked to each student _____ .

4. Your _____ opinion is important to me.

differ
different
differently
difference

5. We do things very _____ .

6. What _____ does it make?

free
freely
freedom

7. May I speak _____ ?

8. You are _____ to do whatever you want.

simple
simply
simplify
simplification

9. I know a _____ solution to the problem.

10. I think that I need to _____ my life.

D. Speaking

DIRECTIONS: *Answer the following questions in class and share your ideas with a classmate or with the class.*

1. Do you know of any religions similar to the one mentioned in the timed reading?

2. What is your opinion of the situation? Do Alice's parents have the right to try to kidnap her from the group or don't they? What would you do in this situation?

3. Does your country have an official religion? Do you know of any official religions of countries of the world? What are the countries and the religions?

4. What is your religion or the religion of your parents? What are the beliefs of this religion?

5. Do you celebrate any religious holidays? What are they? How do you celebrate them?

E. Writing

DIRECTIONS: Combine the following sentences. Use one of these words: although, because, therefore, however. There are two possibilities for each sentence.

Examples: I took a heavy sweater. It was cold.

I took a heavy sweater because it was cold.

It was cold. Therefore, I took a heavy sweater.

1. I am allergic to aspirin. I never take it.

2. I hate cold weather. I live in a cold climate.

3. Some friends of mine came over last night. I couldn't study.

4. I was very sick. I went to school.

5. It was supposed to rain. I took my umbrella.

6. I don't like to study. I realize it is important to study.

7. He went to the doctor's. He was feeling sick.

8. It seems like a waste of time. I'm going to do it anyway.

Look Back

A. Vocabulary

DIRECTIONS: Circle the letter of the choice that best completes each sentence.

1. I don't know very much about his ____, but his present behavior is more important to me.

    a. autonomy   b. background   c. authority

2. The biggest part of a group of people is the ____.

    a. minority   b. majority   c. population

3. What is the ____ for the marriage between two religions or races?

    a. term   b. intermarriage   c. portion

4. I am not ____ that this is the best way to solve the problem.

    a. considered   b. apparent   c. convinced

5. Stealing is a ____.

    a. kidnap   b. crime   c. brainwashing

6. My ____ idea is the same as yours; we just disagree about the details.

    a. unsuccessful   b. local   c. basic

7. There is no ____ between the different living areas of the house. It is all one big room.

    a. discrimination   b. separation   c. independence

8. Which church do you ____ in?

    a. worship   b. head   c. occur

9. No one else thinks he is handsome, but in my opinion he is very ____.

    a. attractive   b. accepted   c. reluctant

10. He is a very ____ teacher; he has taught for fifteen years.

    a. autonomous   b. official   c. experienced

B. Matching

DIRECTIONS: Find the word or phrase in column B which has a similar meaning to a word in column A. Write the letter of that word or phrase next to the word in Column A.

A	B
1. _____ tolerance	a. idea
2. _____ apparent	b. take a person by force
3. _____ occur	c. acceptance
4. _____ separation	d. because
5. _____ concept	e. self-government
6. _____ belief	f. word
7. _____ local	g. obvious
8. _____ term	h. happen
9. _____ kidnap	i. principle
10. _____ since	j. split
11. _____ autonomy	k. near

Answer Key

Section 1: **A.** 1. 2 2. 5 3. 4 4. 1 5. 3 6. 6 7. 7 **C.** a. 3 b. 6 c. 5 d. 1 e. 1 f. 4 g. 2 h. 5 i. 1 j. 7 **D.** 1. similar 2. different 3. similar 4. similar 5. different 6. similar 7. similar 8. different 9. different 10. similar 11. similar 12. different 13. different 14. similar 15. similar **E.** 1. a 2. a 3. b 4. c 5. b 6. b 7. a 8. c 9. a 10. b

Section 2: **A.** 1. b 2. a 3. a 4. c 5. b 6. c 7. c 8. a 9. a 10. b **B.** 1. b 2. a 3. b 4. c 5. c 6. c 7. b 8. a 9. b 10. c

Section 3: **A.** 1. T 2. ITK 3. F 4. ITK 5. F 6. T 7. T 8. ITK 9. T 10. T **B.** 1. c 2. a 3. b 4. b 5. a 6. c 7. a 8. b 9. b 10. a **C.** 1. generally 2. generalize 3. individually 4. individual 5. differently 6. difference 7. freely 8. free 9. simple 10. simplify **E.** 1. I am . . . aspirin. Therefore, I . . . or Because . . . aspirin, I . . . 2. I . . . weather. However, I . . . or Although I . . . weather, I . . . 3. Some . . . night. Therefore, I . . . or Because . . . night, I . . . 4. I was . . . sick. However, I . . . or Although . . . sick, I went . . . 5. It was . . . rain. Therefore, I . . . or Because it . . . rain, I . . . 6. I don't . . . study. However, . . . or Although I . . . study, I . . . 7. He went . . . because he . . . or He was . . . sick. Therefore, he . . . 8. It seems . . . time. However, I . . . or Although it . . . time, I'm . . .

Section 4: **A.** 1. b 2. b 3. a 4. c 5. b 6. c 7. b 8. a 9. a 10. c **B.** 1. c 2. g 3. h 4. j 5. a 6. i 7. k 8. f 9. b 10. d 11. e

chapter 14

A Changing America

A First Look

A. Main Idea

DIRECTIONS: *Before you begin to read, look at these main ideas. There is one main idea for each paragraph. Write the number of the paragraph next to the main idea of that paragraph. Work* very *quickly. Do not read every word at this point.*

1. _____ the era of complacency

2. _____ the cold war

3. _____ a return to realism

4. _____ the importance of the individual

5. _____ an uncertain future

6. _____ protest in the 1960s

7. _____ new social and moral issues

B. Reading

DIRECTIONS: *Now read carefully.*

        World War II was a turning point in the United States: In-   *1*
numerable changes have taken place since that time. Immediately   *2*
after the war and into the 1950s, Americans enjoyed the security   *3*
1   of victory. Families were growing and production was expanding.   *4*
The 1950s was a time of complacency, for "taking things easy." The   *5*
war was over and it was a time of peace. Americans were proud of   *6*
their victory; life seemed problem-free. This carefree life did not last   *7*
long, however.   *8*

        The launching of Sputnik, the first satellite put into orbit,   *9*
ended the 1950s abruptly. The calm was gone, and Americans be-   *10*
2   came concerned with Russian power and technological advances.   *11*
They had to keep up with the Russians. The cold war, the undeclared   *12*
conflict between the United States and the Soviet Union, was here.   *13*

An even more drastic turning point which jolted Americans out of the complacency of the 1950s was the assassination of President Kennedy in 1963. This marked the real division between the two eras. Protest erupted everywhere, tearing at the established traditions. Blacks protested against racism. Martin Luther King began this movement with peaceful demonstrations, but increased tension resulted in riots in many large cities and in the subsequent assassination of this peaceful leader in 1968. There was also protest against the war in Vietnam. War had never been so close to Americans; they experienced it on television, in their own living rooms. For the first time, Americans questioned the government about the necessity of war.

The 1960s also brought drug experimentation and the discovery of the pill, a new form of birth control. American society faced moral and social issues unheard of ten years before. Many dramatic changes took place, and a new idealism evolved. People truly believed that if they worked together, they could change the "system."

But as the 1970s began, Americans realized that the government was incapable of making quick changes. People had spent a great deal of time and energy with few results. They realized that they had very little control over the government, particularly after the Watergate coverup under the Nixon administration. Individuals began to use their energy and power for themselves. Getting a good job, moving ahead, and living comfortably became priorities. Americans became so self-centered that the ten years between 1970 and 1980 have often been called the "Me Decade."

This feeling of inadequacy and impotence was also evident internationally: Americans withstood the high prices for oil, witnessed Russian imperialism, and were outraged at the capture of American hostages in Iran. They began the 1980s uncertain about America's position in the world. They once thought that they could have everything, do everything, and be everything. With diminishing energy sources and increased terrorism, Americans started to become more realistic.

Americans do, indeed, face many uncertainties but somehow feel that everything will be O.K. Perhaps the pioneer spirit, which built the country, will also help Americans change, improve, and adapt to their future.

Reading Clue

14.1 "Getting" (36) is the ____ in the sentence.
      (a) subject
      (b) verb
      (c) adjective

Look at page 224 for the answer.

C. Scanning

DIRECTIONS: Write the number of the paragraph where you find the following information.

a. _____ a time for taking things easy

b. _____ Americans experience war

c. _____ a new idealism

d. _____ the government incapable of making quick changes

e. _____ Americans, jolted out of complacency

f. _____ the cold war

g. _____ drug experimentation

h. _____ priorities

i. _____ Americans face many uncertainties

j. _____ increased terrorism

D. Vocabulary

DIRECTIONS: Look at the following pairs of words. Find the word on the left in the reading.
Compare its meaning to the word(s) on the right. Are the words similar or different?
Write similar or different on the line.

innumerable (1-2)	few	1. _____
victory (4)	loss	2. _____
complacency (5)	nervousness	3. _____

carefree (7)	relaxed	4. _____
launching (9)	takeoff	5. _____
satellite (9)	space ship	6. _____
undeclared (12)	unspoken	7. _____
drastic (14)	dramatic	8. _____
jolted (14)	shocked	9. _____
erupted (17)	exploded	10. _____
tearing (17)	ripping	11. _____
riots (20)	peaceful demonstrations	12. _____
coverup (35)	expose	13. _____
priorities (37)	unimportant items	14. _____
evident (40)	uncertain	15. _____
inadequacy (41)	inability	16. _____
withstood (41)	experienced	17. _____
witnessed (41–42)	observed	18. _____
outraged (42)	complacent	19. _____
realistic (47)	impractical	20. _____

E. Reading Comprehension

DIRECTIONS: Circle the letter of the choice that best completes each sentence.

1. The 1960s are considered a decade of ____ .
   - a. self-centeredness
   - b. complacency
   - c. protest

2. The author says that the pioneer spirit ____ .
   - a. is realistic
   - b. made America
   - c. has a certain future

3. The 1950s could *not* be called an era of ____ .
   - a. security
   - b. protest
   - c. pride

4. The author mentions ____ assassination(s).
   - a. an
   - b. several
   - c. two

5. The launching of Sputnik ____.

   a. changed the attitude   b. was in 1950   c. made Americans proud
      of Americans

6. People probably worked together more during the ____.

   a. 1950s   b. 1960s   c. 1970s

7. The author mentions ____ events which moved the 1950s into the 1960s.

   a. several   b. two   c. three

8. A decade lasts ____ years.

   a. ten   b. one-hundred   c. twenty

9. ____ was *not* an example of an international problem.

   a. Watergate   b. High oil prices   c. The capture of the hos-
                                                          tages in Iran

10. The *national* turning point between the 1950s and the 1960s was ____.

   a. the launching of   b. the eruption of protest   c. the death of America's
      Sputnik   leader

section 2

Look Again

A. Vocabulary

DIRECTIONS: Circle the letter of the choice that best completes each sentence.

1. Marriage is a(n) _____ in life.

   a. launching   b. turning point   c. outrage

2. I am very _____ my son's achievements. He is a wonderful child.

   a. evident about   b. proud of   c. drastic about

3. She must be angry; she left the party _____ without saying goodbye.

   a. inadequately   b. realistically   c. abruptly

4. If she continues to take drugs, the results could be _____ .

   a. incapable   b. drastic   c. undeclared

5. The explosions _____ everyone in the office.

   a. marked   b. erupted   c. jolted

6. Animals must be able to _____ in order to survive.

   a. realize   b. adapt   c. keep up

7. You are always dreaming; you have to become more _____ .

   a. idealistic   b. realistic   c. evident

8. Who _____ the accident?

   a. outraged   b. realized   c. witnessed

9. Someone has to make the decision for him. He is _____ doing it himself.

   a. diminishing   b. incapable of   c. self-centered

10. Two cars and a house in the suburbs are _____ for some Americans.

    a. morals   b. priorities   c. self-centered

B. Reading Comprehension

DIRECTIONS: Circle the letter of the choice that best completes each sentence.

1. A very important priority in the 1960s was ____.

   a. birth control   b. changing the system   c. experimentation

2. In the 1960s, people believed in the power of the ____.

   a. group   b. individual   c. system

3. The Vietnam War was different from previous wars because Americans ____.

   a. understood it clearly   b. watched it on TV   c. knew that it was
                                                                 necessary

4. Americans lost faith in their government after ____.

   a. the race riots   b. the assassination   c. Watergate
                                 of Kennedy

5. ____ was an example of social change.

   a. The pill   b. High prices for oil   c. Diminishing energy
                                                                 sources

6. Martin Luther King ____.

   a. led riots   b. increased racial tension c. was killed

7. The author feels that Americans are now more ____ than in the 1960s.

   a. practical   b. idealistic   c. positive

8. The 1950s lifestyle was abruptly shocked ____.

   a. after the war   b. because of protest   c. at the death of Kennedy

9. The author mentions ____ types of protest during the 1960s.

   a. two   b. three   c. several

10. The author mentions ____ priorities for the 1970s.

   a. two   b. three   c. several

C. Questions

DIRECTIONS: Answer the following questions.

1. What important events moved the 1950s into the 1960s?

2. Describe some aspects of the 1960s which the author mentions. What other ideas do you know about from your own experience?

3. Explain some of the differences between the 1960s and 1970s.

4. How do Americans feel in the 1980s?

5. Of course, all the events which took place in the United States during this period, since World War II, are not in this article. Name some other events that you are familiar with and explain why these events were important.

Contact a Point of View

A. Timed Reading

> DIRECTIONS: Read the following point of view and answer the questions in four minutes.

People often ask me, "What do you think is really important in the United States?" I really think that independence is one of the most important American values. From childhood we learn to be independent, to think for ourselves, to stand on our own two feet. American society insists that its young people be independent; therefore, it should not be surprising when young people move away from their families at eighteen or nineteen years of age. Of course, not all young people leave home at eighteen, nor do most parents want their children to leave. However, living independently from one's family is an accepted part of the American value system.

Large business firms also encourage this separation of the family. Organizations often transfer their employees to other states and even to other countries. This mobility is important for people who want to improve their job opportunities. I know a lot of people who leave their home and friends for professional reasons. It is not uncommon to have brothers and sisters living in different areas of the country, far from each other. Americans feel the loss of a sense of belonging because they don't know exactly where home is. This loss of belonging, alienation, is a common ailment in American society. For most people, the traditional hometown is a thing of the past.

Because they don't know where they belong, people tend to look out for themselves. Many of the best-selling novels insist that *You Are Number One*, that you should *Watch Out for Yourself*, and other such titles which encourage you to think about yourself first. Thinking about yourself is valid, but some people don't leave enough room to think about other people. Sometimes divorce, separation, or termination of relationships are easy solutions to difficulties. The very need to be independent, which Americans value so greatly, can also result in a feeling of intense alienation and isolation. In this impersonal society, a delicate balance must be found.

DIRECTIONS: *Read each of the following statements carefully to determine whether each is true, false, or impossible to know. Check the appropriate blank.*

	TRUE	FALSE	IMPOSSIBLE TO KNOW
1. Independence is part of the American character.	_____	_____	_____
2. Mobility is often important professionally.	_____	_____	_____
3. Many Americans don't leave their hometowns.	_____	_____	_____
4. American society encourages independence.	_____	_____	_____
5. "Alienation" is a need to be independent.	_____	_____	_____
6. Most parents want their children to leave home.	_____	_____	_____

	TRUE	FALSE	IMPOSSIBLE TO KNOW
7. According to the author, too much independence can have negative results.	———	———	———
8. There are many books about divorce and separation.	———	———	———
9. The author thinks that living independently is a good idea.	———	———	———
10. *Home Is Where the Heart Is* is a best-selling novel.	———	———	———

B. Vocabulary

DIRECTIONS: Circle the letter of the word(s) with the same meaning as the italicized word(s).

1. I am not worried about him. He *can stand on his own two feet.*

   a. understands easily   b. values independence   c. relies on himself

2. She *insists* that you spend the night.

   a. doesn't want   b. looks out for   c. suggests strongly

3. I want to become a movie director; *therefore,* I go to the movies almost every day.

   a. although   b. so   c. however

4. She *encouraged* me to go to the university.

   a. jolted   b. influenced   c. asked

5. I was *transferred* to the Florida office.

   a. adapted   b. moved   c. pushed

6. This city is very *impersonal.*

   a. warm   b. cold   c. friendly

7. That conflict marked the *termination* of diplomatic ties between the two countries.

   a. continuation   b. inception   c. conclusion

8. Your argument is *valid,* but I don't agree.

   a. worthwhile   b. honest   c. interesting

9. Most people feel a sense of *alienation* when they experience culture shock.

   a. sadness   b. not belonging   c. homesickness

10. He was *completely* unaware of the other people in the room.

a. very   b. totally   c. really

C. Word Forms

DIRECTIONS: Choose the appropriate word form for each sentence.

1. evident
   evidently

2. drastic
   drastically

3. necessary
   necessity
   necessarily

4. peace
   peaceful
   peacefully

5. Formal
   Formality
   Formally

6. victory
   victorious

7. quick
   quickly

8. real
   reality
   really

9. support
   supportive
   supportively

10. alienate
    alienation

1. It is _____ that she knows him very well.

2. The results of this political decision could be _____ _____ .

3. He is not _____ the most important person here.

4. We hate this war: We want a _____ end to it.

5. _____ style is important in business letters.

6. We must be _____ over cancer.

7. The salesman answered me _____ and walked away.

8. What is the _____ of the situation?

9. Those parents _____ their children's decisions.

10. _____ is a fact in our technological society.

D. Speaking

DIRECTIONS: Choose four or five of the following events which have greatly changed life in your country during the last twenty years. Share your ideas with a classmate or the class.

Political

_____	war (international)
_____	civil war
_____	political protest
_____	riots
_____	assassinations

Economic

_____	new trade benefits
_____	low exportation
_____	inflation
_____	tax

Social

_____	changes in family structure
_____	drugs
_____	new sexual freedom
_____	changes in traditional male/female roles

How do people in your country feel about these changes?

What are some of the fears of people in your country?

What are some of the hopes for the future?

Is the atmosphere in your country positive or negative? Has it changed over the last twenty years?

Optional

DIRECTIONS: *Prepare a brief (five-minute) speech about your country. Explain some of the current history and then talk about the attitudes now. Conclude with a look toward the future.*

E. Writing

DIRECTIONS: *Prepare the presentation in exercise D in written form. Divide your writing into three distinct divisions: introduction (explain to the reader what you are writing about), body (explain the facts and information about your country), and conclusion (review your ideas and close).*

Look Back

A. Vocabulary

DIRECTIONS: Circle the letter of the choice that best completes each sentence.

1. What are your reasons for going there? Do you want good weather or a good university? What are your ____.

   a. realizations   b. priorities   c. influences

2. ____ people often have impractical ideas.

   a. Realistic   b. Idealistic   c. Successful

3. It is ____ that he doesn't understand. Take a look at him.

   a. dramatic   b. secure   c. evident

4. That waitress was very ____ with me. She didn't say "Good morning."

   a. inadequate   b. abrupt   c. outraged

5. If he gets a new car, I want a new car. I have to ____ with him.

   a. declare conflict   b. become concerned   c. keep up

6. There must be two ____ at a marriage.

   a. couples   b. witnesses   c. parents

7. He is very sick. I'm sorry to say that his strength is ____ quickly.

   a. diminishing   b. expanding   c. increasing

8. The president of the company was taken ____. The terrorist demanded $2 million.

   a. assassinated   b. hostage   c. unheard

9. The thief was captured and ____ put on trial.

   a. drastically   b. realistically   c. subsequently

10. He always thinks about other people. He's not at all ____.

    a. self-centered   b. complacent   c. carefree

B. Matching

DIRECTIONS: Find the word in column B which has a similar meaning to a word in column A. Write the letter of that word next to the word in column A.

	A		**B**
1. _____	drastic	a.	war
2. _____	powerless	b.	terrible
3. _____	abruptly	c.	true
4. _____	try	d.	selfish
5. _____	carefree	e.	unrealistic
6. _____	idealistic	f.	impotent
7. _____	complacency	g.	casual
8. _____	real	h.	self-satisfaction
9. _____	self-centered	i.	experiment
10. _____	military conflict	j.	suddenly

Appendix

READING CLUES

1.1
page 4

Such as introduces (b), an example. *For example* is another way to give an example.

> *I like winter sports such as skiing and ice-skating.*
> *I get a lot of exercise in the winter. For example, I ice-skate and ski.*

For more information about writing these expressions, see the writing exercise on page 13–14.

2.1
page 19

Except for introduces one item which is different from a number of other things.

> *I get up early every day except for Sunday.*

For more information, look at the writing exercise on page 28–29.

2.2
page 19

But usually separates two ideas which are different from each other.

> *I speak Spanish well, but I speak French very poorly.*

For more information, look at the writing exercise on page 28–29.

3.1
page 34

A colon (b) introduces explanations, examples, or groups of examples.

> *There was a lot of fruit in the basket: apples, oranges, bananas, and peaches.*
> *There are three problems: people, time, and money.*

3.2
page 35

Writers often use (b) a comma before the explanation of a word, an expression, or a name.

> *George Washington, the first President of the United States, led the American army during the Revolutionary War.*
> *Cottage cheese, a soft white cheese made from skim milk, is popular with people on diets.*

4.1
page 49

i.e. introduces an explanation of an idea.

> *His work was inconsistent; i.e., he sometimes did it very well; at other times he did not even do it.*

5.1
page 65

First, then (second), after that, *final,* or *finally* introduce a sequence or progression.

> *First I went to the store, then I went to the bank, and finally, I was able to eat some lunch.*

6.1
page 81

Words such as *rarely, rare, few, seldom, hardly ever,* and *too* have (a) negative meanings.

> *It's too far to walk. Let's take a bus.*
> *There are few people on the streets at 3:00 A.M.*

6.2 page 81	*Without* shows negation. *It is difficult to read without using a dictionary.* (verb + ing)

6.2
page 81

Without shows negation.

> *It is difficult to read without using a dictionary.*
>
> (verb + ing)

7.1
page 96

Reasons (a) or causes follow the word *because.*

> *We didn't have the picnic because it rained.*

8.1
page 113

Obviously and *of course* introduce ideas which the writer assumes are common knowledge (known by all readers) but wants to emphasize.

> *Obviously, <u>Contact U.S.A.</u> is about the United States.*

9.1
page 129

The author believes that this expression is false, i.e., that the United States is not a land of opportunity for all people. Writers sometimes put quotation marks around expressions to be sarcastic, to show that they do not believe them.

> *The American "dream" is to have a house in the suburbs.*

10.1
page 145

However introduces a contrast in ideas.

> *I left my house early. However, the traffic was terrible and it took me a long time to get here.*

11.1
page 161

Although introduces (b), an idea different from the rest of the sentence, a contrasting idea.

> *Although he was very tired, he studied all night.*

For more information about using *although*, see the writing exercise on pages 172–173.

12.1
page 178

In addition to and *furthermore* introduce (a), additional ideas. *In addition to* introduces a noun or pronoun. *Furthermore* and *in addition* introduce sentences with subjects and verbs.

> *In addition to tuition, there are food, housing, and transportation expenses.*
> *The apartment was in a dangerous neighborhood, it needed paint, and furthermore, the rent was high.*

13.1
page 194

As opposed to and *whereas* show contrast. *As opposed to* is used before nouns. *Whereas* is followed by a complete sentence with a subject and verb.

> *Try Brand X as opposed to Brand Y.*
> *I always study in the morning whereas my husband studies at night.*

13.2
page 194

Since introduces (c) a reason.

> *Since I am feeling tired, I am going to go home early.*

14.1
page 210

Getting is (a), the subject of the sentence. The *-ing* form of the verb, the gerund, is used as a noun, as the subject or object in a sentence.

> *Studying history can be boring.*
> *Knowing how to speak another language is important.*
> *I really like swimming.*

REVIEW TEST 1

DIRECTIONS: *Circle the letter of the choice that best completes each sentence.*

1. Cotton is a ____ of farms in the south.

   a. product   b. lifestyles   c. work

2. What kind of ____ is necessary to be a truckdriver?

   a. issue   b. institution   c. knowledge

3. I don't know the city at all, but there is an ____ center to help me.

   a. advertisement   b. impression   c. information

4. What ____ of life in the city is difficult for you? Is it the noise?

   a. lifestyle   b. aspect   c. entertainment

5. The study of English ____ studying pronunciation, grammar, and other things.

   a. alters   b. forms   c. includes

6. I never ____ my teachers. They are always right.

   a. question   b. hear   c. form

7. I am in a difficult ____. I don't know what to do about it.

   a. problem   b. situation   c. entertainment

8. Crime is ____ poverty.

   a. typically   b. proud of   c. associated with

9. I don't know the answer. ____ it is "B."

   a. Perhaps   b. Typically   c. Immediately

10. This TV has a terrible ____. It is very unclear.

    a. image   b. custom   c. inflation

11. I asked a policeman for ____.

    a. language   b. assistance   c. problems

12. What is your educational ____? Did you go to high school?

    a. background   b. religion   c. place

13. The ____ of the building is unwilling to help us.

    a. neighborhood   b. division   c. owner

14. If you do not have your book, ____ another student.

    a. belong to   b. share with   c. compare

15. Protestantism is a ____ in the United States.

    a. religion　　　　　　b. downfall　　　　　　c. chance

16. I am fine ____ one thing; I have a headache.

    a. such as　　　　　　b. generally　　　　　　c. except for

17. My children don't like to study, but I ____ them to do it.

    a. force　　　　　　b. call　　　　　　c. divide

18. What ____ do you live in?

    a. neighborhood　　　　　　b. opportunity　　　　　　c. religion

19. Problems between blacks and whites are ____ problems.

    a. religious　　　　　　b. political　　　　　　c. racial

20. A weekend with an American family is a good ____ to learn English.

    a. mixture　　　　　　b. opportunity　　　　　　c. freedom

21. What are the ____ of studying in the United States?

    a. reflections　　　　　　b. advantages　　　　　　c. concepts

22. This drink doesn't ____ any whiskey, does it?

    a. entertain　　　　　　b. benefit　　　　　　c. contain

23. His business is doing well. It's ____ .

    a. conflicting　　　　　　b. spacious　　　　　　c. prosperous

24. He is very sick and will never leave the hospital. He is ____ .

    a. revitalizing　　　　　　b. dying　　　　　　c. improving

25. In a mirror you see a(n) ____ .

    a. value　　　　　　b. reflection　　　　　　c. aspect

26. Sports is a form of ____ .

    a. entertainment　　　　　　b. conflict　　　　　　c. revitalization

27. A doctor is a(n) ____ , but a waitress is not.

    a. job　　　　　　b. executive　　　　　　c. professional

28. She lives in the ____ of Chicago.

    a. cities　　　　　　b. suburbs　　　　　　c. space

29. Let's discuss everything about this problem, all ____ .

    a. chances　　　　　　b. benefits　　　　　　c. aspects

30. My friends ____ old furniture.

    a. retire   b. restore   c. develop

Test Items	Chapter
1–10	1
11–20	2
21–30	3

REVIEW TEST 2

DIRECTIONS: Circle the letter of the choice that best completes each sentence.

1. Because she gets up early, she always ____ .

    a. takes her time   b. rushes   c. hurries

2. You only have two ____ to choose from: Do it or not.

    a. essentials   b. advantages   c. alternatives

3. The TV is a(n) ____ of knowledge.

    a. source   b. impression   c. waste

4. I like you very much. Your ____ is important to me.

    a. well-being   b. imperfection   c. routine

5. It is ____ to study the verbs of a language.

    a. essential   b. certain   c. immense

6. It is ____ for a man to stay home and take care of the children.

    a. commonplace   b. traditional   c. unusual

7. ____ is an important factor in automobile accidents.

    a. Waiting   b. Speed   c. Waste

8. He's ____ in the music world.

    a. well-being   b. well-known   c. ironic

9. His ability in English is ____; he understands almost nothing.

    a. immense   b. perfect   c. minimal

10. He was born here. He's ____ .

    a. a native   b. foreign   c. a stranger

11. That doctor is a(n) ____ in cancer treatment.

    a. position   b. specialist   c. identity

12. You are ____ these problems. They can't be real.

    a. missing   b. looking at   c. imagining

13. The President's ____ of office is four years.

    a. term   b. sense   c. role

14. What is your ____ in this company?

    a. factor   b. form   c. position

15. I don't know this city; it is ____ to me.

    a. unfamiliar   b. negative   c. paranoid

16. The policeman helped me ____ my problem.

    a. solve   b. create   c. experience

17. I was ____ to hear about his death; he seemed healthy and young.

    a. unreasonable   b. positive   c. shocked

18. I am not ____ to cooking for myself, so I'm not eating well.

    a. self-conscious   b. accustomed   c. successful

19. It is not a big problem; just a small ____ will solve it.

    a. adjustment   b. service   c. escape

20. We have our ____ exam at the end of the course.

    a. final   b. resulting   c. technological

21. In my ____ job, I made a lot of money, but I didn't enjoy it.

    a. partial   b. traditional   c. previous

22. In the word *establish* you ____ -sta- when you speak.

    a. emphasize   b. support   c. tell

23. This project ____ too much work. I don't want to do it.

    a. involves   b. centers   c. increases

24. I don't have the ____ , but I am sure that there are more married women under thirty than men.

    a. statements   b. statistics   c. sociology

25. I don't feel well. I am not ____ American food yet.

    a. depending on   b. tending to   c. accustomed to

26. People move all the time here. It is a ____ area.

    a. transient   b. traditional   c. private

27. Smoking is a bad ____ , but I can't stop it.

    a. support   b. reaction   c. habit

28. Don't wear formal clothes. You can dress ____ .

    a. personally   b. basically   c. casually

29. I have to ____ public transportation because I don't have a car.

    a. be accustomed to   b. depend on   c. support

30. University ____ are usually fairly liberal.

    a. communities   b. traditions   c. frequently

Test Items	Chapter
1–10	4
11–20	5
21–30	6

REVIEW TEST 3

DIRECTIONS: *Circle the letter of the choice that best completes each sentence.*

1. I can't ____ to go out to dinner twice a week; it's too expensive.

    a. provide   b. volunteer   c. afford

2. How do you ____ this word? I can't find it in the dictionary.

    a. influence   b. define   c. respond to

3. It's ____ to try to meet the plane. It arrives in ten minutes.

    a. sure   b. useless   c. serious

4. I have three children. With my salary it's impossible to ____ .

    a. make ends meet   b. get discounts   c. use my savings

5. He is retired; ____ , he is no longer working.

    a. because   b. therefore   c. but

6. He has ____ problems. It's his back.

    a. financial   b. physical   c. emotional

7. Soap is a ____ .

    a. food   b. necessity   c. fuel

8. I ____ help, but he didn't want any.

    a. took   b. got started   c. offered

9. He is happy to retire. He has a positive ____ about retirement.

    a. influence   b. benefit   c. attitude

10. A little concern can ____ many problems.

    a. spend   b. ease   c. build

11. If my boss doesn't give me a(n) ____ soon, I'm going to quit my job.

    a. fire   b. employee   c. raise

12. I have a lot of good work experience; I'm definitely ____ for this job.

    a. qualified   b. discriminated   c. employed

13. My salary is not ____; I need to get a new job.

    a. adequate   b. financial   c. wealthy

14. I ____ my secretary because she couldn't type and was often late to work.

    a. quit   b. fired   c. hired

15. Women are in the ____ in engineering programs; there are more men.

    a. minority   b. ambition   c. majority

16. I can't ____ this medicine will help you but I think it will.

    a. value   b. prevent   c. guarantee

17. I ____ to go to that restaurant again. It's terrible!

    a. prevent   b. refuse   c. succeed

18. That company treats its ____ well.

    a. employees   b. employers   c. classes

19. His father thinks he should ____ a lawyer.

    a. succeed   b. concept   c. contact

20. My ____ is in electronics, but I am now in computers.

    a. prejudice   b. background   c. application

21. I don't want to talk to him, but he is always calling me. He is very ____.

    a. advantageous   b. blatant   c. persistent

22. In the United States, racial issues are usually ____ with blacks.

    a. ironic   b. associated   c. designated

23. If you become a member of the club, your ____ at weekly meetings is essential.

    a. inequality   b. heritage   c. participation

24. The committee ____ her the winner.

    a. segregated   b. excluded   c. designated

25. He made every ____ to win the contest.

    a. attempt   b. gain   c. benefit

26. In 1973, the court decided this problem, but it ____ its decision in 1980.

    a. segregated   b. succeeded   c. reversed

27. It is ____ to smoke in elevators according to the law in some states.

    a. unjust   b. illegal   c. discriminatory

28. She always talks too much at parties, so I ____ her from the guest list.

    a. excluded   b. qualified   c. reversed

29. He is ____ to teach French.

    a. adequate   b. qualified   c. adapted

30. Some people who smoke feel that smoking sections in restaurants are ____ .

    a. affirmative   b. discriminatory   c. ironic

Test Items	Chapter
1–10	7
11–20	8
21–30	9

REVIEW TEST 4

DIRECTIONS: Circle the letter of the choice that best completes each sentence.

1. We have to copy the paragraph but make changes. The paragraph is a ____ .

    a. model   b. position   c. factor

2. The newest ____ makes use of computers.

    a. salary   b. capability   c. technology

3. Sun and water both ____ to healthy plants and trees.

    a. contribute   b. differentiate   c. return

4. Something strange happened to me this morning, but it was an interesting ____ .

    a. lifestyle   b. experience   c. status

5. We agreed on our positions and duties, and we were all happy with the ____ .

    a. role   b. tradition   c. arrangement

6. We just joined the club; we are new ____ .

    a. heads   b. members   c. positions

7. I know nothing about it; I have never ____ this problem before.

    a. encountered   b. demanded   c. supported

8. I don't want to ____ your decision, but I really think you should listen to me.

    a. support   b. adjust   c. influence

9. I ____ your decision. I think that you are right.

    a. support   b. differentiate   c. influence

10. I think that I am going to leave my job because it is not ____.

    a. capable   b. satisfying   c. reinforced

11. I ____ your opinion.

    a. repair   b. agree with   c. consist of

12. She is not happy with her husband. She always ____ him.

    a. complains about   b. conflicts with   c. discriminates

13. When is your paper ____ in this class?

    a. qualified   b. provided   c. due

14. He never carries an umbrella, even if it is raining. He is ____.

    a. impractical   b. hostile   c. typical

15. Equal rights for women is an important ____ in the United States.

    a. issue   b. ethic   c. solution

16. Your salary ____ your experience.

    a. supports   b. depends on   c. varies

17. Every month I prepare a ____ to cover all my expenses.

    a. bill   b. budget   c. belt

18. The electricity isn't working, so that light is ____.

    a. additional   b. repaired   c. useless

19. She is a wonderful woman. She ____ only the best.

    a. angers   b. depends on   c. deserves

20. Often people have to have a car. It is a ____.

    a. convenience   b. necessity   c. complaint

21. I promise to end discrimination and, ____, stop prejudice.

    a. however   b. without   c. furthermore

22. We ____ gas at 3:00 this morning.

    a. misused   b. realized   c. ran out of

23. The word *ghetto* ____ from Italian.

    a. guesses   b. depends   c. derives

24. He cannot cash that check. He has ____ funds in his account.

    a. additional   b. insufficient   c. limitless

25. You have to insulate the house to save ____ .

    a. effects   b. waste   c. heat

26. Gas produces ____ .

    a. energy   b. fuel   c. erosion

27. If you have the flu, aspirin offers some ____ .

    a. protection   b. relief   c. solution

28. I am not interested in international politics. I'm only interested in ____ politics.

    a. foreign   b. domestic   c. world

29. Oil is limited; ____ , we must find other sources.

    a. therefore   b. but   c. furthermore

30. He never comes on time. Don't ____ him.

    a. differentiate   b. derive   c. depend on

Test Items	Chapter
1–10	10
11–20	11
21–30	12

REVIEW TEST 5

DIRECTIONS: Circle the letter of the choice that best completes each sentence.

1. The federal government has little control over state taxes; in taxes, the state is ____ .

    a. hierarchical   b. tolerant   c. autonomous

2. The teacher ____ grammar because he thought it was the most important thing.

    a. tolerated   b. emphasized   c. controlled

3. The child was ____ and held until his parents paid a lot of money for his return.

    a. kidnapped   b. joined   c. absent

4. I like history very much; something about it really ____ me.

    a. convinces   b. brainwashes   c. attracts

5. I am ____ to say yes, but I will because you want me to accept.

    a. protestant   b. reluctant   c. considering

6. The invention of the transistor was a ____ in the field of communications.

    a. basis   b. principle   c. breakthrough

7. There was no ____ announcement, so no one paid any attention to the new rule.

    a. official   b. head   c. principle

8. ____ I am interested in traveling, I always go to movies about other countries.

    a. Whereas   b. Since   c. Though

9. Fruit is one ____ of food.

    a. category   b. separation   c. member

10. How do you ____ special holidays?

    a. assist   b. worship   c. celebrate

11. Before you begin a new project, you should determine your ____.

    a. reluctance   b. priorities   c. complacency

12. It is ____ that women are in better physical condition than men; they live longer.

    a. realistic   b. evident   c. official

13. The problem of drug addiction is growing, not ____.

    a. expanding   b. diminishing   c. becoming

14. He was a(n) ____ to the assassination; he saw the whole incident.

    a. person   b. witness   c. official

15. The ____ of the ocean liner, Queen Elizabeth II, was a momentous occasion.

    a. turning point   b. launching   c. division

16. At first I thought that he understood, but after a few minutes I ____ that he didn't.

    a. mentioned   b. withstood   c. realized

17. His mother was ____ by the bad language of his friends.

    a. moved ahead   b. diminished   c. outraged

18. A decade ____ ten years.

    a. experiences   b. lasts   c. tears

19. He always speaks ____ ; I wish he would be practical.

    a. realistically   b. idealistically   c. subsequently

20. ____ he is an intelligent person, he doesn't express himself well.

    a. So   b. However   c. Although

Test Items	Chapter
1–10	13
11–20	14

Diagnostic Chart

CHAPTER	SECTION 1 A C D E	SECTION 2 A B	SECTION 3 A B C E	SECTION 4 A B	Number of Mistakes
1					
2					
3					
Review Test					
4					
5					
6					
Review Test					
7					
8					
9					
Review Test					
10					
11					
12					
Review Test					
13					
14					
Review Test					

0-5 (mistakes) = Excellent
6-10 = Good
11-15 = Review chapter
16 (or more) = Do chapter again